THE WITHERING ROAD

THE WITHERING ROAD

BY: KADESH SANDERS

Studio of Books LLC
5900 Balcones Drive Suite 100
Austin, Texas 78731
www.studioofbooks.org
Hotline: (254) 800-1183

Ordering Information:
Special discounts are available on quantity purchases by corporations, associations, and others. For details, contact the publisher at the address above.

Printed in the United States of America.

ISBN-13: Softcover   978-1-970283-25-9
           eBook   978-1-970283-26-6

Table of Contents

PROLOGUE

In the once-prosperous nation of New Egypt, a shadow crept across the land. What had once been a beacon of faith and morality slowly descended into decadence and sin? Streets that once echoed with hymns and prayers now resounded with the clamor of vice and indulgence.

The shift began subtly. They enacted policies, and these policies eroded the foundations of traditional values. Leaders encouraged a new freedom, one that dismissed the old ways as outdated. Temples stood empty, their once vibrant congregations now found in taverns and pleasure houses.

People cast aside the sanctity of life, which caused murder rates to climb. Fornication became a public spectacle, celebrated rather than condemned. Smoke from illicit substances filled the air, mingling with the stench of moral decay. Alcohol flowed like water, drowning the sorrows of a people who had lost their way.

The government, once a bastion of justice and righteousness, now passed laws that mocked the divine. They promoted greed, corruption, and indulgence, all in the name of progress. Those who dared to speak out were silenced, their voices drowned in the cacophony of a society that had turned its back on its creator.

As the nation spiraled deeper into sin, the heavens grew silent. God removed the protection that had once shielded New Egypt, leaving the people vulnerable to their own devices and the consequences of their choices.

It was then that the storm clouds gathered, and the winds of judgment stirred, foreshadowing the trials that were to come.

The invading Belvarian leader's speech began, "My fellow citizens and esteemed allies, today we stand on the brink of a new era." "An era where our great nation, fueled by our unwavering resolve and unmatched strength, will rise to heights never imagined."

"The land before us is rich with untapped resources, resources that rightfully belong in the hands of those who have the vision and the will to claim them. Our enemies have squandered their wealth, living in decadence, while we have endured. But no more!"

"It is time to unite under our banner, to take what is ours, and to secure a future where we, the strong and the righteous, prevail."

"Our cause is just. Our mission is clear. Let us march forward and claim the destiny that awaits us!"

The echoes of boots striking the marble floor fill the Grand Hall of Belvaria as Supreme Chancellor Varik Thalor stands on an elevated platform, surrounded by towering banners bearing the emblem of the Belvarian Empire. Behind him, vast formations of soldiers march into position, their armor gleaming under the crimson sky. Massive war machines rumble across the land, their engines growling like hungry beasts.

A holographic transmission displays the worried faces of diplomats and leaders from neighboring nations, their voices overlapping with anxious demands.

International Leaders (Various Nations)

Prime Minister of Novaria: "Chancellor Thalor, we demand to know why your armies are mobilizing along our borders?"

President of Terranova: "This level of military buildup is unjustified. Are you preparing for an invasion?"

Empress of Aldoria: "Are you intending to seize resources from our lands? Answer us, Thalor!"

Chancellor Varik Thalor (Belvarian Leader)

(laughs, shaking his head as he slowly steps forward toward the holographic display)

"Oh, my dear colleagues, how predictable you all are, always scrambling, always questioning. "Why are your armies moving?" "What is your intent?" "Foolish. Look at you all of you clutching your pearls while the tide of history rises before you."

What did you expect? That I would sit idly by while lesser nations squander their wealth? That I would ask permission to take what is rightfully ours?

(He turns to his generals, nodding approvingly as columns of soldiers tighten their formations and tanks roll forward.)

Your questions amuse me, truly. Do you ask the lion why it stalks its prey? Do you question the storm as it gathers in the sky?

(His tone darkens, his voice carrying a sharp, commanding weight.)

"No. You cower. Make your preparations. You should kneel.

"You already know the answer, and yet you ask. Why do I gather my forces? The goal is to correct the imbalance. To claim what should have been ours long ago. To strip the weak of what they do not deserve."

(He leans in, voice dropping to a chilling whisper.)

And when the steel of Belvaria marches upon your lands, when your cities burn, and your banners fall… remember that you had your answer all along."

He cuts off the holographic transmission with a flick of his wrist.

In the dimly lit command bunker of Belvaria, the air was thick with tension as high-ranking officials gathered around a large, glowing map of New Egypt. The room was silent except for the steady hum of machinery and the occasional rustle of papers.

At the center stood General Aldric, his face set in grim determination. Around him, a team of officers and technicians monitored the situation, their eyes flickering between screens and instruments.

General Aldric: "Is everything in place?"

Technician: "Yes, General. All systems are ready. The missiles are ready to launch, awaiting your command.

General Aldric: "Patch me through to the sub-team."

A brief crackle of static, then the voice of the sub-team leader, Major Ivanov, came through the speakers.

Major Ivanov: "General, we are in position. All launch systems are green."

General Aldric took a deep breath, knowing the weight of the decision he was about to make.

General Aldric: "Proceed with the countdown."

Major Ivanov: "Yes, sir. Beginning countdown. Ten… nine… eight…"

In the bunker, everyone held their breath as the numbers ticked down, each second stretching into eternity.

Major Ivanov: "…three… two… one… Launch."

Missiles launched, their deadly payloads arcing into the sky, and a series of lights blinked on the control panels. A silent hush fell over the room as the screens showed their trajectory, heading toward New Egypt.

General Aldric: "God help us all."

The room was silent, the gravity of their actions hanging heavy in the air.

In the aftermath of the launch, General Aldric and his team watched the screens with a mix of anticipation and trepidation. They braced for the next phase after launching the missiles.

An officer turned to the general. "Sir, reports confirm that they have disabled all coastal defense systems," the officer said.

General Aldric nodded, his expression unyielding. "Good. Make sure the paratroopers are ready. We strike at the heart of their defenses before they can regroup." "We have complete control of the airspace and surrounding waters."

In the adjacent room, the flight commanders were issuing last instructions to the troops who would soon parachute into the heart of New Egypt. They meticulously crafted the placement of the chaos and conf, establishing a foothold in the regions untouched by the initial strikes.

Major Ivanov: "All units, prepare for deployment. Our target is the capital. We expect minimal resistance, but stay vigilant. This is our moment to seize control."

The tension was palpable as the paratroopers boarded their planes, the hum of engines rising as they prepared to take off.

In the aftermath of the nuclear strikes, a heavy cloud of regret hung over the allied leaders and generals. They had placed their trust in Aldric, only to realize too late the true extent of his madness. Now, with the devastation wrought by their actions, they found themselves trapped in a nightmare of their own making.

As the news of the strikes spread, the leaders gathered once more, their faces etched with guilt and despair.

Ally Leader: "What have we done? We followed a madman, and now we've unleashed horrors we can't control."

Another general: "We thought it was a strategic move, but it was a trap. We've given our power to a man who seeks only destruction."

The realization of their complicity gnawed at them, but they knew there was no turning back. To resist now would mean facing Aldric's wrath, a fate none of them dared to contemplate.

General Aldric's brutality manifested, and the once-united coalition now stood on shaky ground. The world watched in horror as the consequences of their actions unfolded, and many wondered how such a catastrophe could have happened.

In the chaos, the people of New Egypt grappled with the devastation. Their country, once vibrant and full of life, was now a battleground, and survival became their only priority.

As the dust settled, the question remained: how did it come to this? The answer lay in the unchecked ambition of a leader who cared little for the consequences of his actions, and the complicity of those who enabled him.

Now, the people had to survive in this new world, clinging to hope and resilience in the face of overwhelming darkness.

And in the ruins of New Egypt, amid ash and fire, only one truth remained for the people:

Survival was all that remained.

Hope became dangerous. Trust became rare.

And the road ahead, The Withering Road,

had only just begun.

CHAPTER 1

THE DAY THE SKY BURNED

Hours earlier, the smell of eggs and toast filled the kitchen. Bridget stood at the stove in her robe, gently flipping a pancake while humming softly to herself. Sunlight filtered through the blinds, casting golden stripes across the counter.

"Mom, I want extra syrup!" Maya called from the table, already swinging her legs in her chair.

"You always want extra syrup," Ethan muttered, half-smiling as he took a bite of his toast.

"I'm growing. Unlike you," Maya shot back with a grin.

Bridget chuckled. "Alright, alright—no syrup wars at the table, please. You're both growing, even if Ethan's just stretching up and not out."

Ethan rolled his eyes. "Thanks, Mom. Appreciate the vote of confidence."

Robert stepped into the kitchen, already dressed in his fishing gear. "Smells amazing, hon." He leaned over, kissed Bridget on the cheek, then grabbed a plate. "Breakfast of champions before I battle the sea."

"Oh please," Bridget teased, "you're just going to nap in the boat with a pole in your hand."

Robert grinned. "It's called strategy."

The kids laughed. Bridget placed pancakes in front of Maya, then ruffled Ethan's hair as she passed. "You two behave today. And help each other, okay?"

"Where are you going again?" Maya asked between bites.

Bridget grabbed her coat from the chair. "There's a new job opportunity in the city. It's just a few days. I'll be back before you even miss me."

Ethan raised an eyebrow. "That's not possible. Maya misses you if you take longer than a Target trip."

"Do not!" Maya huffed.

Robert stood and walked Bridget to the door. "Are you sure you want to drive today? I can drop you at the station."

Bridget smiled. "I'll be fine. It's just a couple of hours out. You go catch dinner. I'll call you tonight."

He kissed her again, longer this time. "I love you."

"Love you, too."

As the door shut behind her, Ethan grabbed the remote. "Alright, let's see what's on."

He flipped through a few channels—cartoons, news, a cooking show.

"…tensions continue to rise as the foreign naval fleet moves closer to—"

Click.

"Ooooh, let's watch Laser Shark Ninjas!" Maya squealed.

Ethan groaned. "You always pick that."

"And you always complain and watch, anyway."

He smirked, then tossed a pillow at her. "Fair."

They both laughed, unaware that the faint voice of the news anchor was already long forgotten.

Everything felt normal.

For now.

Back in the living room, Ethan lounged sideways on the couch, head halfway off the edge, while Maya sat criss-crossed on the floor, still watching their favorite show.

"You know," Ethan said, tossing a cushion into the air and catching it, "if you ever stopped watching this show, the world might stop spinning."

Maya snorted. "You mean the world would be boring without my excellent taste."

Ethan gave her a sideways glance. "You've watched this same episode like… five times."

"Yeah, and I still laugh every time Laser Shark does that flying kick thing."

He smiled. "Okay, that part's kind of cool."

Maya turned and leaned against the couch. "You're not that bad, you know. For an annoying brother."

Ethan sat up and nudged her with his foot. "And you're not that bad either for a sister who always hogs the remote."

Before she could fire back, the TV screen suddenly froze, then went black.

A loud, steady beep filled the room.

BEEEEEP.

Maya jumped. "What the—?"

The screen flickered to a black background with white text. This is a test of the Emergency Alert System. This is only a test.

A computerized voice followed, flat and emotionless.

"This is a test of the Emergency Alert System. Considering the rising global tensions, this is a scheduled regional broadcast. Please remain calm and follow the instructions given by the authorities."

Ethan muted the TV. The silence in the room felt heavier than the alert itself.

Maya looked over at him. "Was that real?"

He shook his head. "Just a test… I think."

"Why now?"

Ethan didn't answer. He was still staring at the screen.

Outside, the wind pushed softly against the trees. Somewhere far off, a dog barked.

Cut to…

Robert Out on the Water

The small boat bobbed gently on the waves. Robert sat back in his folding seat, rod resting across his knees, eyes closed under his cap.

The sun shimmered over the water, but there was a stillness that didn't sit right.

He cracked one eye open and noticed the seagulls circling erratically closer to shore than usual.

Pulling out his phone, he checked the time. No missed calls. No messages.

Still… something felt off.

He reeled in his line slowly, watching the horizon.

Bridget On the Road

Bridget hummed along to the music playing from her phone as she cruised down the highway, her overnight bag on the passenger seat.

The city wasn't far now—maybe an hour left.

She reached to adjust the volume when the music suddenly cut off. Static crackled from her speakers before the same computerized voice from the TV kicked in.

"This is a test of the Emergency Alert System. This is only a test."

She furrowed her brow and tapped the screen. The message played again, then silence.

"Okay… that's weird."

Bridget's eyes drifted to the rearview mirror, then back to the road.

She didn't know it yet, but this was the last normal day any of them would ever know.

The salty breeze rolled over the deck of the fishing boat as Robert gripped the edge, squinting into the horizon. The water stretched out like a sheet of glass, broken only by the rhythm of waves and the gentle bob of the vessel beneath his boots.

"Hey, Robert!" the deckhand called out to an older man with a sunburnt face and a cigarette tucked behind his ear. "You see that shadow under the port side?"

Robert stepped over, his eyes sharp. "Could be a school. Or something big."

They worked quickly; the crew moving with the ease of years spent doing this dance. Ropes creaked, the winch hummed, and together they hauled in the net. Water splashed high, glistening in the sunlight, and then the net broke the surface.

"Holy —" one guy blurted. "That's the biggest dang cod I've ever seen — 180 pounds!"

Fish flopped and thrashed as the net hit the deck. A massive silver-scaled cod, nearly four feet long, lay at the center, flailing its tail.

Robert grinned widely, breathless for a second. "Get a picture of that beast before we clean it."

The guys laughed, and someone was already pulling out their phone. There was joy at the moment — simple, earned, and honest.

As the crew settled, Robert leaned on the railing, letting the sea wind hit his face. His mind drifted, just for a second, to Bridget and the kids. He could still see Maya making a syrupy mess and Ethan tossing that pillow.

He smiled.

Bridget stepped into the hotel lobby with a suitcase in one hand and a leather folder in the other. The hotel wasn't fancy, but it was clean, modern, and quiet—perfect for a business trip.

The receptionist handed her a key card. "Room 367. " The elevator is to your right."

"Thanks." She tucked the card into her purse, walking toward the elevator with a little bounce in her step.

Once in her room, she unpacked her overnight bag and pulled out her pressed blazer, hanging it neatly on the closet door. She had laid out her makeup on the counter, and her shoes lined up near the bed, with everything arranged just the way she liked it.

She glanced at a framed photo on her phone — Robert, Maya, and Ethan grinning in front of the old oak tree in their backyard.

"I miss you guys already," she whispered, her voice warm.

Her phone buzzed. A message from Robert.

Caught a monster today. Kids would've flipped. Love you.

She smiled, typed back quickly.

Can't wait to hear all about it. My interview is in 3 hours. I'm so nervous. Love you more.

She sat at the edge of the bed, staring at the clock. Three hours felt like both a blink and a lifetime. Her palms were already sweaty, her heart beating a little faster than usual.

This job—it meant everything. A chance to grow. A chance to help her family.

She stood up, took a deep breath, and whispered, "You've got this."

But somewhere in the back of her mind, she couldn't shake the sound of that emergency alert from earlier.

Ethan lay sprawled on the couch, lazily flipping channels while Maya stood at the fridge door, scanning the shelves.

"Hey," Ethan called out, eyes still on the screen, "grab me some orange juice?"

"Say please," Maya teased, pulling out the carton with a smirk.

Ethan sighed. "Please."

She closed the fridge with her foot, walking toward the living room just as the TV screen blinked to black again.

BEEEEEEEEP.

They both froze.

The same computerized voice returned—but this time, the tone was different. Sharper. Urgent.

"This is not a test. This is not a test. We have detected multiple nuclear strike missiles above New Egypt. We advise you to seek immediate shelter. If you have a basement, go there now; or if you have a nearby parking garage, go there now. If you are in a skyscraper, go to the middle floors. Gather batteries, a flashlight, food, water, and a radio to hear government messages. Foreign troops are invading. Please engage. Repeat—this is not a test."

Maya's fingers loosened. "No way!" The orange juice slipped from her hands, hitting the floor with a thud, the cap popping off and spilling across the tile.

"Ethan…" she whispered, her voice cracking.

He shot up from the couch, eyes wide, heart thudding in his chest.

"They said it's not a test," Maya said, trembling.

Ethan didn't even look back. "Dad's at the docks. We have to run!"

Without another word, they bolted out the front door, barefoot on the porch, sprinting through the neighborhood street. Every step was a blur of fear and adrenaline.

Birds shot into the sky. A siren screamed in the distance.

Then—silence.

Ethan turned his head slightly.

A flash—bright, blinding—lit the sky behind them.

"Don't look back!" he shouted, grabbing Maya's hand.

The surrounding air trembled.

A thunderous boom ripped through the atmosphere, causing it to appear the sky itself had torn in half.

The shockwave hit moments later—deafening, powerful, knocking them to the ground. But by some miracle, they'd both instinctively done everything right.

Mouths open. Ears covered.

Still alive.

But nothing would ever be the same.

The world was a blur of ringing and dust.

Ethan pushed himself up, blinking through the haze. "Maya!" he shouted, but he couldn't even hear his own voice. His ears were ringing so loudly that it felt like the world had gone silent.

Maya was on the ground beside him, dazed, her hands still over her ears. Tears streamed down her cheeks, but she nodded when he grabbed her arm.

They got up, legs wobbling, lungs burning.

And they ran.

Their feet scraped the pavement like chalk on a sidewalk. The sky had turned an unnatural shade of orange, and the light behind them glowed like a second sun on the horizon.

Ethan glanced once over his shoulder—just once.

A column of smoke and fire climbed into the sky. They watched as a wall of destruction, fueled by 12 megatons of nuclear power, obliterated the city they knew from 15 miles away.

But he turned back to Maya, his grip tightening on her hand.

"We're gonna find Dad," he mouthed.

And they kept running.

As they stumbled through the ash and broken light, Ethan coughed and tried to steady his breathing. His ears still rang like distant bells, but the sharpest edge of it had dulled.

Maya's voice cracked through the silence, barely more than a whisper, but clear enough for him to hear.

"I can't believe we're alive…"

Ethan looked at her, eyes wide, dirt smeared across her face, hair tangled by the wind.

She blinked slowly, tears in her lashes. "If we survived… that must mean we have a reason to live. If God spared us…"

Her voice faded for a second, but Ethan saw something in her eyes—something strong.

He nodded, still holding her hand. "Then we'd better not waste it."

And they ran faster toward the shore. Out on the water, Robert stood near the stern of the boat, wiping sweat from his brow as the rest of the crew laughed and bragged about the monster catch.

Then it hit.

The shockwave. The sound.

The light.

It flared on the horizon, far beyond the coastline—too bright, too fast, too wrong. It painted the clouds in a twisted shade of white-gold and orange.

"Robert," one sailor whispered, "what the hell is that?"

He didn't answer.

A low rumble rolled over the water a few seconds later. It was deep, like the groan of a waking giant.

Robert's gut clenched.

He dropped the rag in his hand and stepped forward, eyes locked on the growing cloud in the distance.

That was toward home.

Toward his kids.

His heart thundered louder than the sky.

"We have to get back," he said, his voice hoarse. "Now."

The captain was already on the radio, shouting for dock control.

Robert didn't wait. He was already at the edge of the deck, gripping the railing, watching the smoke rise.

"I'm coming," he whispered to no one.

To everyone.

To his family.

Robert gripped the edge of the boat tighter as the cloud climbed higher, curling into the sky like a monster made of smoke and flame.

The captain's voice crackled over the handheld radio. "Dock's down. No contact. Emergency services are experiencing heavy traffic."

Robert turned sharply. "Then they abandoned us."

The crew looked at him, stunned.

"We're under attack," he said, eyes never leaving the horizon. "That wasn't an accident. That was a nuclear strike."

"Jesus save us!" one of the younger deckhands whispered.

Robert clenched his jaw. "Thank God we're alive. But I've gotta go. My kids are out there."

The captain stepped forward. "Robert, wait—what are you gonna do?"

Robert grabbed his gear, slinging it over his shoulder in one quick motion. "I don't know. Run. Move. Just don't stop."

He looked each of them in the eye. "If you see more flashes, don't look. You stare at one of those, and you'll go blind. Head down. Mouth open. Cover your ears."

The captain nodded slowly. "Good luck, man."

Robert gave a nod back. "Get to your families. All of you."

And then he leapt onto the dock, dropping everything, and took off at full sprint, boots pounding the wood, heart racing harder than it ever had before.

He didn't know how far he had run, or how long it had taken.

But then—

He saw them.

His children, Maya and Ethan, were running down the street. Covered in dust. Face tight with panic.

Already heading toward him. They'd seen the sky light up, heard the sirens, and knew where to find their father. They collided with each other halfway, relief momentarily washing over them.

"Maya! Ethan!"

They froze, then turned.

"Dad!" Maya and Ethan screamed. "It's gonna be alright!" Robert replied.

Robert caught them both in his arms, pulling them in so tightly it felt like the world could break apart and he'd still be holding them together.

"You're alive," he breathed, voice shaking. "You're alive…"

Ethan clung to his shirt. "We saw it, Dad. The entire sky lit up."

"I know," Robert said, holding the back of Maya's head. "But you did everything right. You bolted. You survived. You found me."

He pulled back just enough to look them in the eyes.

"We're staying together now. No matter what. Alright?"

They both nodded.

And the three of them turned together—toward the smoke, the unknown, the road ahead.

But they weren't alone.

Not anymore. The front door swung open with a loud creak, and Robert guided Ethan and Maya inside with urgency.

The house was still standing—quiet, untouched—but it no longer felt like home. It felt like a shelter, a checkpoint, a moment to breathe before the world came crashing down again.

"Shoes off. Track nothing in," Robert said, his voice steady but tight.

The kids didn't argue. They slipped off their shoes, hands trembling, and tear-stained faces still in shock.

Robert went straight for the hallway closet, pulling it open to reveal a shelf packed tight with vacuum-sealed meals, jugs of water, first aid kits, and a worn backpack already half-packed.

"I need both of you to listen," he said, kneeling and unzipping a side pocket. "No questions right now. We're going to move fast, and we're going to move smart."

He reached up and pulled down a Ziplock bag with dried seaweed and a bottle of iodine tablets.

"Take these," he said, handing two tablets and a strip of seaweed to each of them. "They help protect your thyroid from radiation. You chew the seaweed, swallow the pill. It might taste like trash, but it'll keep you alive."

Maya gagged slightly at the bitterness. "Dad, what if Mom…"

He paused.

He didn't want to shut her down. But he couldn't fall apart.

Not now.

Robert looked at her, eyes glassy, jaw clenched. "We don't know what happened to her. But if she's alive—and I believe she is—she'll be doing the same thing. Fighting to survive."

He stood, dashing to the back of the closet, unlocking a metal case. Inside: a handgun, a hunting rifle, and a box of ammunition.

Ethan started. "You were really ready for this…"

Robert nodded. "I prayed I'd never have to be. But I wasn't gonna be caught off guard."

He stuffed essentials into the pack—water, dry food, medical supplies, flares, a flashlight, extra batteries, and a compass. Everything had a place.

"We can't take it all," he muttered, more to himself than to them. "Just what we need. Just enough to make it." Go take a quick shower to wash the radiation off your skin and change clothes so you don't turn into a monster," Robert ordered! Yes, Dad, Maya and Ethan replied, running upstairs quickly. "10 minutes, kids, we need to move now! Maya and Ethan quickly returned downstairs, anxious about what comes next.

Maya looked up at him, eyes wide. "What about Mom?" she asked, her voice trembling.

Robert took a deep breath. "We don't know right now. But we have to be strong. We're going to find her."

He turned to Ethan, handing him a flashlight and a pocket knife. "You keep this close. Only use it if you have to."

Then to Maya, a small emergency whistle and a flare pen. "If we get separated, use this. Only once. I'll find you."

They nodded, eyes wide with fear but slowly grounding in his calm.

Robert glanced around the room one last time—the photos on the wall. The toy train is still sitting in the corner. Bridget's scarf is on the coat rack.

He didn't let himself linger.

"We leave in ten minutes. Grab warm clothes, good socks, and anything you can carry. We don't know what we'll run into. But we move together. Got it?"

Both kids answered quietly. "Got it."

Robert looked toward the window, the sky still choked with a reddish glow.

His heart ached. As they left the house, reality set in. Their home, once a place of safety, was now just a memory as they ventured into the unknown.

But his hands stayed steady.

They were going to survive. They had to.

In a city miles away, Bridget sat in a sleek office, her thoughts on the job interview that had just concluded. She was hopeful about the opportunity—finally, a chance to contribute to her family's future. But as she exited the conference room, a television screen in the lobby caught her eye.

The breaking news ticker read: "Nuclear Explosion Near Coastal City." Bridget's heart sank as images of smoke and devastation filled the screen. She instinctively touched the phone in her pocket, but she knew that calling might be futile. The city under attack was near their home and her husband's workplace.

Conflicted, Bridget watched the scenes unfold. She struggled between hoping for the new job opportunity and dreading what she felt. If her family was gone, what did any of this matter? Yet, she couldn't give up hope. Bridget stayed put for the moment, knowing that leaving the city might put her at risk or make it harder for her family to find her.

She steeled herself, whispering a silent prayer for their safety and for the strength to navigate the days ahead.

Bridget's hands trembled as she dialed her husband's number. Each ring that went unanswered tightened the knot in her stomach. The phone left behind in their rush lay silent in their empty home.

As the call disconnected, Bridget's manager burst into the office, his face pale. "We have to evacuate now! The country is under nuclear attack and invasion. Nowhere is safe." His words pierced through her panic.

They hurried to the elevator, joining a crowd of anxious employees. As the doors closed and they descended, a deafening explosion rocked the building. A ballistic missile had struck.

The elevator doors opened onto a scene of chaos. Flames and smoke billowed from the upper floors, and the building's structure groaned under the impact. Bridget and her colleagues rushed through the lobby, dodging debris as they reached the street.

Outside, they looked up to see the building's top floors engulfed in flames, the structure beginning to collapse. Bridget's heart pounded—not just from fear but from the realization that she needed to survive, for her children, her husband, and herself.

As Bridget rushed out of the building, the war zone transformed the cityscape. Explosions echoed around her, and smoke and fire filled the sky. Amidst the chaos, she caught sight of military transport planes flying overhead, soldiers parachuting down into the city. The friendly soldiers moving swiftly began directing people to safety.

Bridget's heart pounded as she ran, but her high-heeled business shoes caught on the uneven pavement, sending her sprawling to the ground. The shock of the fall, combined with the overwhelming fear and uncertainty, paralyzed her. Tears welled up as she sat on the pavement, the weight of the moment crashing down.

A soldier, noticing her distress, rushed to her side. "Ma'am, we have to move. We're here to help." He extended a hand, his voice calm but urgent.

Bridget looked up, her eyes meeting his. She nodded, took a deep breath, and let him help her to her feet. The soldier guided her toward a gathering point, where others were already being evacuated.

As the soldier helped Bridget to her feet, the sound of gunfire erupted nearby. She turned to see paratroopers, who had seemed like their rescuers moments before, opening fire on the soldiers and civilians alike. Chaos broke out as people screamed and ran for cover.

Bridget's heart raced as she tried to stay low, her eyes searching for an escape. The crowd surged around her, and she stumbled forward, her mind a blur of panic and fear. In the confusion, she lost sight of the soldier who had helped her, and the sounds of gunfire grew louder.

A sudden burst of bullets whizzed past, and Bridget felt the ground beneath her give way as she fell. The world spun, and for a moment, everything seemed to slow.

Amidst the smoke and noise, her vision blurred.

As the chaos unfolded, Bridget's vision swam, the world around her blurring into confusion. The paratroopers' gunfire rained down, and she saw soldiers and civilians alike falling. Her mind raced, but her body wouldn't respond.

At that moment, everything slowed down. The sounds of gunfire became muffled, and the surrounding cries faded. Bridget stumbled, her breath caught in her throat, and her vision faded to black.

The last thing she saw was a mixture of smoke and the blur of figures moving in the distance before darkness took over.

The city square, once bustling with life, now lay in a state of eerie stillness. Civilians and soldiers lay scattered on the ground, the aftermath of the brutal attack. Smoke billowed from nearby buildings, and the sounds of distant gunfire still echoed through the air.

Beneath a layer of debris and dust, Bridget lay motionless, her eyes closed. The camera in the narrative pans out slowly, capturing the scene as if it were a tableau of tragedy. The dust settles around her, making it unclear whether she is merely unconscious or worse.

Bridget's eyes fluttered open as she stood with the help of her boss. In the surrounding chaos, she saw visions of her family—her son, daughter, and husband—standing together, smiling as if nothing had changed. The warmth of that vision gave her strength, reminding her of what she was fighting for.

But reality quickly shattered the moment. The sound of soldiers shouting and more gunfire erupted as troops descended on their position. Bridget instinctively ducked, but the enemy shot her boss again, and he collapsed beside her. Bridget's vision blurred once again as she felt something hit her, too, and everything around her seemed to slow down. Blood dripped from her mouth and side.

CHAPTER 2

THREEFOLD CORD

Robert and his family walked for about five miles when they heard the sound of heavy military vehicles.

Robert said, "Stay out of sight, kids. Get down by the fence. Maya and Ethan duck against a wooden fence as Robert peeks over it. Suddenly, Robert hops onto the fence to get a closer look.

He helped his children climb over the fence quickly. "Wait here," Robert said as they approached the back door. Still staying as quiet as possible, using hand signals and eye contact. A kind elderly lady and her son opened the door. Hello, Margaret invited me to come in. I have some fresh lasagna. She exclaimed, the kids look hungry. "Yes, we haven't eaten lunch yet," Maya and Ethan replied. Thank you, Margaret, for helping us Robert said, somewhat confused and relieved. Hello, sir, what's your name? Hello, I'm Adrian, and I'm going to resist this occupation. Margret, don't talk nonsense; you'll get yourself killed. "Mom, I have to do this; I have to live on my feet, not on my knees," Adrian shouted. "I know, but be smart; you don't have a group yet. Suddenly, military MRAPs and transport trucks roll down the street. " Everyone, come out with your hands up. We don't want to hurt you. You can come with us, and we'll give you food, water, medical care, and shelter. If you resist, you will be subject to deadly force!" the Belvarian Occupation loudspeaker blurred. Adrian grabs his rifle and runs out, taking aim and shooting a soldier on a turret. "For freedom," Adrian shouted as Belvarian occupation troops shot him down. "Nooo, my son," Magret wails as she mourns. "Step away from him, ma'am. I'm sorry, but he fired on us," the soldier replied. "What you shouldn't even be here in our country, you're killing our people. Go to hell! "You need to calm down unless you want to be next the soldier suggested. The troops loaded every on to the trucks. Sam, tag and bag the two bodies, Roger that. Maya and Ethan vomited after seeing their first two deaths. Robert also comforted them because he was unsettled, too. "I know this is hard, but do not show fear; they feed off it." Cling, cling. Gunfire erupted as 50 resistance fighters attacked the convoy. The convoy crashed, and 45 occupational troops died in just 15 minutes. "Hello, "I'm here to rescue you. A recruit pinged us, and we tracked the convoy. May he rest in peace, Adrian," the resistance fighter said. "We'll give him a proper burial — a genuine hero for his country. "See, kids, I told you we'd be fine. Maya and Ethan smiled.

The old military base had once been a hub of life—barracks full of soldiers, mess halls echoing with chatter, drills on the yard. Now, it was a stronghold for what remained of the resistance forces, scarred but holding strong.

Robert, Maya, and Ethan sat at a metal table in what used to be the officer's lounge. The room smelled of old paper, oil, and cold coffee. Across from them sat a resistance captain—a calm, tired man in his forties with sharp eyes and a map rolled out in front of him.

"You've been in the dark a long time," he said, pointing to red-marked zones across the map. "You're not the only ones."

Robert leaned in, arms crossed. "So what exactly happened?"

The captain exhaled slowly. "Months of tension led up to it. We thought it'd be a cold war—just threats, posturing. But then they struck first. Nuclear, precise, aimed at major military sites and infrastructure. Took out our satellites, bases, comms… not everywhere, but enough to cripple command."

Maya looked horrified. "And no one stopped them?"

"We tried. Some of our jets got in the air. Some of our missiles were launched. But they had planned this for years. It was a shock assault. They hit us… and then they landed."

Ethan sat forward. "You mean they actually invaded?"

The captain nodded. "Ground forces. Special ops. Their dictator planned this perfectly. He calls it 'Reclamation'—as if this country was always his. His soldiers are ruthless, trained for suppression and propaganda. They've taken whole cities without a shot being fired."

Robert glanced at his children, then back to the captain. "What's the resistance doing?"

"We're holding what we can. Liberating towns when possible. But we're scattered. We need leaders, supplies, and communication. Every day we survive is a minor victory."

Silence followed for a moment, the weight of it all sinking in.

Then Maya broke the quiet. "Have… have you seen our mom? Bridget?"

The captain shook his head slowly. "Name doesn't ring a bell. But we've got others still out there. If she's alive, we'll find her."

Robert gave a small nod, though his face stayed tight.

After everything they'd just heard, that was still the only mission that mattered.

They weren't done. Not until they brought their family back together.

Trays clattered softly. The rustle of gear. The low hum of wind over worn-out barracks.

Robert stood at a folding table inside the resistance base's supply depot, his hands tight around a reinforced tactical vest. Beside him, Maya zipped a military-grade backpack with an AK-47 slung over her shoulder, and Ethan inspected a compact M4 carbine rifle with cautious awe. Robert picks an M249 LMG. He slung his hunting rifle over his back and packed ammo in his backpack.

They had food now—proper food. Vacuum-sealed protein, dense calorie bars, canteens full of purified water.

The resistance hadn't just saved them.

They'd rearmed them.

"You're sure you know how to use that?" Robert asked Ethan, nodding toward the rifle.

Ethan looked up, nervous but steady. "You showed me enough. I'll only use it if I have to."

Robert gave a slow nod, pride in his eyes. "That's all I needed to hear."

Maya stuffed the last of the iodine pills into her med pouch and adjusted the straps on her chest rig. "This stuff is heavy."

"You'll get used to it," Robert said. "Or you won't. Either way, you're carrying it."

Maya rolled her eyes but smiled faintly. That spark—they were still holding on to it.

A resistance soldier handed Robert a map, marked with red zones and narrow paths. "You've got maybe three safe miles ahead, then things get gray."

"Appreciate it," Robert said, folding the map and sliding it into his vest.

The kids loaded up. Boots laced, packs secure, eyes hardening with each step closer to the exit gate.

No more safety nets.

Only the road—and the promise of what might lie at the end.

Robert looked back once at the base.

Then, forward to the world beyond.

"Let's move."

The gravel crunched under their boots as they moved down the cracked back road, the resistance base shrinking behind them with every step.

Maya had her pistol tucked into the side pocket of her jacket. Ethan had a compact rifle slung across his back, the strap too loose but holding. They didn't know how to use them—not really. But they knew they had to carry them.

Just in case.

They walked in silence for a long time, the early morning sun barely cutting through the gray ash drifting in the air.

Then Maya stopped.

She didn't say anything. She just stood still… and started to shake.

Robert turned quickly. "Maya?"

She tried to speak, but the words broke on the way out. Her shoulders dropped, and she buried her face in her hands.

"I can't… I just… what if she's not—what if she's not out there?"

Ethan looked at her, and something cracked inside him, too. His breath hitched. Tears welled up fast and fell even faster.

Robert's heart twisted, but he stayed steady. He knelt beside them both, his voice low but firm.

"Hey, listen to me. Look at me."

They did.

"I know you're scared. I am too. But we can't break now. We'll find your mom. I believe that."

He placed a hand on each of their shoulders.

"But belief isn't enough. We have to survive. We have to be strong, or we'll never make it far enough to even know the answer."

Maya sniffed hard and wiped her face. Ethan followed, brushing the tears away with the back of his hand.

They didn't say a word.

But they nodded.

They stood taller.

They adjusted their straps and checked their weapons.

Because wherever Bridget was—alive or not—they were going to walk that road for her.

And they were going to walk it strongly.

The town was a ghost, with crumbling buildings, shattered windows, and silence that felt too heavy to be natural. Weeds split the pavement. Cars sat rusting in the streets like tombstones. As they moved along the empty road, Robert kept one hand near his holster.

Then—

"Hold up," a voice barked.

From behind a burnt-out truck, three men stepped out. Dirty, scarred, armed. Marauders.

The one in front had wild eyes and a bat slung over his shoulder.

"Drop your packs," he growled. "All of it. Weapons too. Do you understand that?"

Maya froze. Ethan's fingers trembled near the strap on his rifle.

Robert stepped forward slowly, placing himself between the kids and danger. "We don't want trouble."

"That's too bad," the marauder sneered. "We do."

But before he could take another step, a deeper voice cut through the tension.

"Stand down."

The man paused, looking over his shoulder, and then someone else emerged from the shadows.

A taller man, older, with a lined face and a calm presence. The leader, Kade.

"Let 'em go," he said.

"What?" the others said in unison. "But—"

"I said Let them go."

His voice was firm. Unshakable.

Robert locked eyes with him. The man didn't blink—just gave a small nod, like he didn't quite understand why he was doing this either.

But something had moved within him.

The marauders stood there, confused and irritated, but obeyed.

Robert slowly led Maya and Ethan past, never turning his back until they were a safe distance away.

Ethan finally whispered, "Why'd he let us go?"

Robert exhaled, his voice low and sure. "Because sometimes… God favors you. Same reason we survived the blast. Same reason those soldiers didn't shoot us on sight. It's not luck."

He glanced at Maya.

"It doesn't mean anything bad will happen. But if it hasn't… it means He's not done with us yet."

Maya's eyes widened.

Those were the words she'd said to Ethan the day of the attack.

She said this phrase before she even knew she believed it.

Now… she did.

The cracked road faded behind them as Robert led Maya and Ethan through a break in the tree line. The woods weren't dense, but thick enough to swallow the highway's noise and erase the marauders from view.

Birds were quiet. The wind creaked through branches like whispers.

Robert paused, checking the direction with a compass he'd clipped to his jacket. "We'll follow the treeline parallel to the highway. Safer this way."

Ethan nodded, rubbing a fresh bruise on his arm. Maya held tight to the strap of her pack, still shaken but focused.

They walked for hours in silence—just the crunch of leaves, the distant sound of a stream, and their breathing.

Eventually, Robert held up a hand.

"Here," he said, pointing to a slight clearing. "We'll camp here tonight. No fire, not yet. But we can eat."

As they dropped their packs, Maya finally sat down and let out a deep, shaky breath. "I feel like we've walked a hundred miles."

"You will," Robert said softly, crouching by his gear. "But you'll get stronger with each one."

He pulled out a small camp stove and a pot.

"Time for a lesson," he said, glancing at Ethan. "Are you hungry?"

Ethan gave a half-smile. "Always."

Robert motioned them closer. "Alright. We're cooking over heat, not flame. No smoke, less chance of being seen. Water first. We purify it with these tablets—watch the count. With too few, you get sick. Too many, it'll taste like bleach."

He guided them through every step—adding powdered soup base, stirring carefully, keeping the pot level.

It wasn't much, but it was warm.

As they ate, the world around them felt a little quieter.

A little more survivable.

And for the first time since the world fell apart... they weren't just running.

They were learning how to live.

Over the next few days in the woods, Robert shifted from protector to teacher.

The fear was still there, but survival had a rhythm now.

In the mornings, he showed them plants—how to identify wild onions, what poison ivy looked like, and how to test unknown berries with a dab on the tongue. "If your lip tingles," he said, "don't eat it. That's your first warning."

Maya was a natural. She picked up on the plant material quickly, her eyes sharp, her fingers careful.

Ethan... not so much.

"Is this good?" he asked, holding up something with three suspicious leaves.

"That'll make your face swell like a balloon," Maya said, smirking.

Ethan dropped it instantly. "I knew that. I was testing you."

They laughed. It wasn't much, but it was the first time in days they'd sounded like themselves.

Later, Robert taught them how to tie snares using sticks and paracord.

Ethan nailed it on the third try.

Maya collapsed the moment she tightened it.

"Oh, come on," she huffed.

Ethan raised a smug eyebrow. "Guess I'm the trap master now."

"Lucky guess," Maya muttered, but her grin betrayed her pride in him.

At night, they sat close, huddled around a flame-free heat source, eating dried soup and telling stories from "before." TV shows, silly fights over cereal, and the way Bridget used to hum when she cooked.

Even in the silence of the woods… There was warmth.

They were still a family.

Changed.

But not broken. It started with a lesson—sticks, twine, carved arrowheads.

Robert showed them how to bend the wood, how to test the tension, and how to notch an arrow just right. It took time.

Ethan picked it up quickly. "It's kind of like aiming with a slingshot," he said.

Maya groaned as her string snapped for the third time. "This is nothing like a slingshot."

But she stuck with it. Eventually, her arrow flew—not far, but it flew.

A few days later, they spotted movement in a clearing.

Deer.

Robert held a finger to his lips and motioned for them to spread out.

Ethan's arrow was clean and swift—his deer dropped instantly.

Maya took three tries, her breathing uneven, but she did it. Her second deer staggered, then fell.

Their cheers were quiet but real.

"We did it," Ethan grinned, chest puffed with pride.

Maya knelt by her deer, heart pounding, overwhelmed but proud.

But then—

A low, chilling growl echoed through the trees.

Robert froze.

Another growl. Then another.

Yellow eyes flickered between the trunks.

Wolves.

But not normal ones. These were gaunt, eyes sunken, patches of fur missing, skin pulled tight and raw in places. Radiation had twisted them.

Robert grabbed the kids. "Run. Now."

They took off through the trees, branches snapping, gear bouncing against their backs.

The growls turned to snarls.

Then—

They saw it. A cave.

They rushed inside without thinking; the darkness swallowed them.

They caught their breath for a split second—then a heavier growl came from the depths.

A shape shifted.

Massive.

Hulking.

A mutated bear rose in the shadows, taller than any normal bear, its fur scorched, one eye missing, muscles rippling beneath cracked skin.

Ethan's breath caught.

Maya whispered, "Oh no…"

Robert stepped in front of them.

Trapped between what chased them…

And something far worse.

The mutated bear roars, shaking dust from the cave ceiling. Robert immediately pushes Ethan and Maya behind a rock outcropping deeper in the cave, keeping low.

Robert knows fighting the bear isn't an option—they're outmatched, and the bows won't stop something that size.

So he scans the cave and sees what might save them: loose rocks overhead near the bear, barely hanging from the ceiling.

He whispers to Ethan, "Light an arrowhead. Use the flint."

Ethan's hands tremble, but move fast. Robert quietly dips the arrow in dried animal fat from their pouch and sparks the flint. Maya steadies his aim.

The bear moves closer.

Ethan fires—thunk!—right above the bear's head.

The flame catches the dry moss and debris.

The cave trembles.

CRACK!

A section of the ceiling gives way.

BOOM!

Rocks collapse over the bear. Dust floods the cave.

The roaring stops.

It's not dead. But it's pinned.

Robert doesn't wait. "Move!"

They dash out the cave entrance just as the wolves catch their scent again—now backing off, afraid of the tremors and the chaos.

The family disappears into the forest.

Hearts pounding. Covered in dirt and ash.

But alive.

Maya, breathless, says, "I thought we were done…"

Robert replies, "So did I. But not today."

That moment solidifies their bond—and shows the reader just how quickly nature has turned.

The smell of cooked venison drifted through the trees like something sacred. For a moment, it didn't smell like survival—it smelled like home.

They'd made it back to camp, dragging the deer carcasses behind them, bruised, shaken, and exhausted… but alive. The woods were quiet now. No mutated growls, no thunder of paws or claws—just the soft crackle of a small, low fire.

Robert stood over the cleaned meat, slicing thin strips and laying them carefully across a flat rock warmed by the fire.

"Now," he said, wiping his hands on a rag, "you don't just eat anything you kill. "You've got to know how to cook it right, or you're spending the night praying to God over a stomachache."

Ethan snorted. "Like that mystery soup in the ration pack."

Maya giggled. "I'm still not convinced that wasn't glue."

Robert smirked. "This'll be better. I packed some salt and pepper before we left home. Had a feeling."

He taught them how to purify the water with tablets, boiling it just long enough to kill the threats but keep it usable for stew and hydration.

Maya stirred the pot carefully. Ethan checked the meat. It smelled… good. Like real food.

Dinner was quiet at first. They were tired. But once the first few bites went down, the conversation opened up.

Ethan made a joke about Maya's deer taking ten arrows. Maya fired back about his "trap master" title not applying to actual aim. Robert laughed harder than he had in weeks—really laughed.

Under the stars, for just a little while, they forgot about the invasion.

They forgot the fear.

They remembered what it felt like to be a family.

Not just surviving.

But living.

As the laughter faded and the fire settled into glowing embers, the surrounding forest grew still again. The warmth of the meal lingered, but the air turned cooler. Softer.

Robert sat back against his pack, arms draped over his knees. Maya leaned onto his side. Ethan poked gently at the coals with a stick, the glow lighting up his face in quiet reflection.

For a while, no one spoke.

Then Robert looked at the pot, still simmering gently, and the scraps of cleaned meat set aside for later.

And he thought—

She used to do this.

Every dinner. Every night. The smell of garlic, the way she'd hum while she stirred. The way she smiled when they said it tasted good, even if it didn't.

He swallowed hard.

Maya shifted beside him. "Mom would've liked this."

Robert nodded slowly. "Yeah. She would've."

"She always made dinner," Ethan added softly. "Even when she was tired."

"She made it feel like everything was normal," Maya whispered.

Robert didn't say anything for a moment. Then he looked at them both.

"She'd be proud of you," he said. "Both of you."

He paused, his voice quieter now.

"And she'd be proud of this. That we're still a family. That we're holding it together."

They sat in that silence—not empty, not heavy.

Just… whole.

Even if she wasn't there, her presence was.

In the fire. In their laughter.

In the food.

She was with them.

And they knew it.

Three weeks had passed since the cave.

The forest had become familiar—still dangerous, but no longer unknown. Robert had taught them well. They knew how to listen now. How to feel when something wasn't right.

So when the growls came again, echoing low through the trees…

They didn't panic.

They moved.

"Grab the flint," Robert said calmly, his voice steady. "Now."

Ethan dropped his bundle of sticks and dug into the side pouch of his pack. Maya unrolled the cloth-wrapped bottle of leftover cooking oil.

"Pour it along the arrow tips. Slow. Even," Robert said. "Wrap a strip of cloth behind the arrowhead. Make sure it sticks tight."

They worked quickly, fingers trembling but focused. The growls grew closer. Faster. Harsher.

Ethan struck the flint.

Spark—spark—swoosh.

The first arrow caught fire. Then Maya's. Then Robert's.

"Up on that ridge," Robert said. "Now. We control the high ground. On my mark, wait for them to break the treeline."

Ethan and Maya nodded, crouching behind a fallen log as their father stood at the center, bow raised, flame flickering at his side like a torch in the dusk.

The brush rustled.

Eyes gleamed.

And then—they charged.

"Now!" Robert yelled.

Three flaming arrows tore through the dark, streaking like falling stars.

The wolves yelped—startled by heat, by light, by pain. One dropped instantly. Another veered off, its shoulder ablaze. The others hesitated.

Maya fired again—her arrow striking one in the flank.

Ethan missed—but the fire scattered them.

And just like that…

They retreated.

Back into the woods.

Back into the dark.

Breathing hard, Maya looked over at her dad. "We won?"

Robert lowered his bow. "No."

He looked at the trees still twitching with movement.

"We survived."

Then he looked at them both, his voice quieter now.

"And we're getting better at it."

The forest had grown too wild, too uncertain.

After the wolves, Robert made the call: it was time to move. The woods had taught them everything they could. The danger was growing… and so was their hunger to find Bridget.

They packed up camp in silence.

Every knot they tied, every arrow they checked, every ration split between them carried weight—not just of survival, but of purpose.

They couldn't take the forest with them.

But they carried the knowledge it gave.

They carried the fire.

And they carried her memory.

Bridget.

They missed her more with every step.

As they stepped back onto the broken road, just past the tree line—

CRACK—CRACK—CRACK!

Gunfire.

"Down!" Robert shouted, grabbing Maya and Ethan and pulling them behind a splintered tree.

Figures emerged fast from the brush—marauders in mismatched gear, some with makeshift armor, others barefaced and desperate.

Their rifles were up, with no hesitation in their eyes.

"I don't care what the boss said!" One of them shouted. "They've got food, weapons—we take it!"

Another voice barked back from the group. "We were told to leave families alone!"

"Then he isn't here, is he?!"

Suddenly, rifles turned inward.

The group erupted in chaos.

Gunfire broke out—at first between them.

Robert didn't wait.

"Get behind that log!" he ordered. "Maya! Bow ready. Ethan—"

Ethan looked down at his pistol, hands shaking.

His first real firefight.

Aimed at people, not creatures.

Maya tried to steady her bow, but she couldn't breathe. She couldn't move.

Her arrow dropped.

"I can't," she whispered.

Ethan's finger twitched on the trigger.

He was terrified.

But when a marauder broke away and charged toward his sister—

BANG!

Ethan fired.

Then again.

The man dropped.

Another one screamed and ran.

Robert fired too, covering their side, focused like stone.

The shootout lasted seconds.

Then—retreat.

The remaining marauders, panicked by their own infighting and Ethan's surprising accuracy, fled into the trees.

Silence returned, broken only by their breathing.

Robert turned to Ethan, who stared at his hands, wide-eyed and pale.

"I… I didn't want to," Ethan muttered.

Robert knelt and cradled his face. "I know. You did what you had to. You saved your sister."

Maya, still holding her bow, dropped it and hugged Ethan tightly.

They weren't ready for this kind of war.

But love—love showed up when fear tried to win.

And that was something no one could take from them.

They thought it was over.

The gunfire had stopped. The woods had gone still again. Robert was just about to check on Ethan's pulse when—

Snap. Crack. ROOOOOAAAAR.

The ground trembled.

From the trees, the remaining marauders came sprinting back—faces twisted in terror, dropping weapons, screaming.

"What the hell—?" Robert turned, eyes narrowing.

And then they saw it.

The bear.

That bear.

The mutated beast that nearly killed them weeks ago—scorched skin, missing eye, massive as a truck and twice as angry—charged through the trees like nature's vengeance itself.

It tore into the marauders without hesitation.

Claws the size of cleavers. Teeth stained with rage.

One man screamed as they lifted him and threw him into a tree like a rag doll.

Another tried to fire—too late.

The rest didn't get far.

The screams echoed. Then stopped.

And the bear turned.

His good eye locked on Robert, Ethan, and Maya.

They stood frozen.

No guns raised.

No bows drawn.

Just silence.

Fear thick as blood.

Maya whispered, "Dad…"

Robert slowly stepped in front of them, his voice low. "Don't move."

The bear sniffed the air—grunted—and took one heavy step forward.

Then…

It stopped.

Its nostrils flared. Its ear twitched. Maybe it remembered them.

Or maybe… it just knew they weren't like the others.

With a final growl, it turned back toward the woods.

And disappeared into the trees.

For a long moment, no one moved.

Then Ethan collapsed to his knees, breathing hard. "Was that real?"

Robert nodded slowly, still watching the treeline.

"Judgment came early for them."

And by grace alone… passed them by.

CHAPTER 3

THE BATTLE OF JERICHO

Robert, Maya, and Ethan approach the quiet outskirts of the town cautiously, tired but alert. Suddenly, Robert gets a prickly feeling on the back of his neck. He slows down.

Somewhere up high… someone's watching.

Then a whistle cuts through the silence.

Robert looks up toward a rooftop, and sure enough—there's a figure aiming down with a rifle.

"Don't move," Paul's voice calls, calm but firm.

Robert squints. "Paul?"

Long pause. Then the rifle lowers. "Well, I'll be damned."

Paul disappears for a second, then comes walking around a corner, rifle slung casually, a small grin tugging at his cheek despite himself.

"Well, you didn't die," he says.

"Sorry to disappoint," Robert replies dryly.

The kids stand awkwardly between them, watching the standoff energy soften just a little.

"Come on," Paul sighs. "You look like someone chewed you up and spit you out. Let's get you off the street."

They settle into a quiet hideout on the edge of town—an old bar Paul's turned into a supply station and lookout.

Over a quick meal, they chatted. Still tense. Still guarded.

Then Paul brings it up.

"The walled city," he says, voice serious now. "You thinking of going there?"

Robert nods slowly. "We're looking for someone. My wife."

Paul leans back, rubbing his face. "Then you need to know—it's not just a city anymore. It's a Warzone. Resistance on one side. Occupiers, on the other hand. And in between?" He looks at Maya and Ethan. "No-man's land. Anyone caught in the middle doesn't walk out."

Robert's jaw tightens.

Paul leans forward, softer this time. "You're gonna need help if you're going in there. Lucky for you… You found me."

And just like that, old grudges fade.

Because survival has a way of healing what pride once broke.

Robert, Maya, and Ethan stood with Paul at the edge of the forest, the distant city skyline barely visible through the haze. Paul pointed to a narrow opening between two collapsed buildings.

"That's the safest route I know," Paul said, his voice low and serious. "The resistance territory is dangerous, but I'll help you get inside. Normally, I'd stay out of this, but for the kids, I'll take the risk."

Robert nodded. "We appreciate it, Paul. Let's gear up. We need to be prepared for whatever's ahead."

Before they moved forward, Robert took Maya and Ethan aside near a small clearing on the outskirts.

"Alright," Robert began, handing them each a rifle. "This is serious. You need to learn how to use these weapons if we're going to make it through the city."

Maya and Ethan listened intently as Robert showed how to hold the rifles, aim, and fire. They practiced for a while, firing at makeshift targets until both felt more confident.

Maya caught on quickly, her focus sharp. Ethan hesitated at first, but eventually steadied his hands and aimed correctly. Robert watched them, pride and concern mingling in his eyes. When they were ready. Paul returned with Pam, who handed them extra vests and gear.

"Let's get moving," Robert said, leading them toward the opening. "Stay close and keep your eyes open."

Robert, Maya, and ten-year-old Ethan sat in the dimly lit room, surrounded by resistance fighters who had become their temporary protectors. The resistance leader, a woman named Maya, explained the situation. "A coalition of nations that have long opposed our country's policies orchestrated the attack. They saw an opportunity to strike. The nuclear attack was just the beginning. They want control."

Maya looked at her father, eyes wide with a mix of fear and understanding. Ethan clutched his backpack, which held the few belongings they had grabbed. Robert, absorbing the gravity of the situation, nodded. "Thank you for explaining. We did not know."

Maya placed a reassuring hand on Maya's shoulder. "We're here to protect you, but we understand if you feel the need to keep moving. It's risky to stay in one place for too long."

Robert looked at his children, then back at Maya. "We need to keep moving. We'll take the supplies and knowledge you've given us, but I can't risk my children's safety. We need to find a place where we can regroup and figure out our next steps."

Maya nodded. "We understand. Stay safe, and know that you're not alone in this fight."

With heavy hearts but determined spirits, Robert, Maya, and Ethan gathered their things and set out once more, their path uncertain but their resolve unwavering.

Would you like to continue exploring their journey or add more depth to this moment?

Let's bring this emotional and intense scene to life, emphasizing Robert's protective instincts and the unexpected mercy shown by the bandits' leader.

As Robert, Maya, and Ethan approached the city where they hoped to find Bridget, their spirits lifted. "We're almost there, guys," Robert said, his voice filled with a mix of hope and relief. "We've come so far. I believe we'll find Mom soon."

Maya smiled, looking at her little brother, Ethan. "Dad's right. We've survived this much. We can do this."

Their optimism was short-lived, however, as a group of armed marauders suddenly surrounded them. "Put your hands up!" one of them shouted, guns trained on the family. "We want your supplies."

Robert instinctively pulled his children close. "Please," he began, his voice calm but firm, "we're just passing through. We've got a couple of kids. Don't hurt us. We barely have anything, just like you."

The marauders' leader, a tall man with a stern expression, shook his head. "That will not cut it." He motioned for his men to move closer.

Robert whispered urgently to his children, "Run!" They darted away as Robert stood his ground, ready to sacrifice himself to protect them.

But before the situation could escalate, the leader raised his hand to stop his men. "Wait," he said, his voice thoughtful. "I don't know why, but I'm going to let this one go." His team murmured in confusion, and he added, "Out of the mercy in my heart for his children."

Robert watched in disbelief as the bandits backed off. He called for Maya and Ethan, who returned to his side, and they quickly continued their journey, the encounter leaving them both shaken and grateful.

As they walked away from the tense encounter, Maya looked up at her father, her brow furrowed with curiosity. "Dad, why did they let us go? They were surely going to hurt us."

Robert paused, taking a deep breath before answering. "That's the mercy of God, Maya," he whispered. God appears in times of great adversity, when we least expect it, and when we think we have lost all hope. The reason the man let us go is that the Spirit of God moved in his heart, telling him not to harm us."

Ethan listened quietly, absorbing his father's words. "So even in the worst times, God is still with us," he murmured, his voice filled with newfound understanding.

Robert nodded, a small smile forming on his lips. "Yes, son. He's always there, guiding us, even when we can't see it. We just have to keep our faith and continue forward."

With this reassurance, they pressed on, holding onto hope as they journeyed toward the city where they hoped to reunite with Bridget.

Maya, with her fiery red hair catching the sunlight, walked with a newfound sense of purpose. The world around her had shifted dramatically, but she felt herself shifting too. Her father's teachings echoed in her mind: survival, faith, and the importance of protecting her brother Ethan.

As they ventured toward the city, Maya's curiosity grew. "Dad," she asked thoughtfully, "I know we have to trust in God, but I also think we need to learn to protect ourselves. If we help ourselves, maybe God will guide us more." Her father nodded, understanding the wisdom behind her words.

Taking her father's old handgun, she felt its weight in her hands. The first shot startled her, but with each round, she grew more accurate and confident. The gun became not just a tool, but a symbol of her determination to protect her family.

The metal grate of a storm drain creaked as Robert slowly pried it open. Beneath them, the storm drain stretched into darkness, a tunnel of cracked concrete and damp air.

Maya peered inside, gripping the straps of her backpack.

MAYA (whispering)

"This is a bad idea."

Robert didn't disagree, but the alternative was worse. Above them, the scavengers still argued, their voices growing more aggressive.

SCAVENGER LEADER (shouting in the distance)

"We move now! Grab everything we can before another gang gets here!"

Ethan swallowed hard, staring into the tunnel.

Ethan (whispering, nervous)

"Are there—things down there?"

Robert didn't answer immediately. Instead, he pulled out a flashlight, clicked it on, and shone the beam inside. The concrete walls were slick; the floor was covered in matted leaves and old debris washed in from storms. But there were no bodies. No footprints.

No signs that anyone had been here recently.

That was good.

Finally, he turned to Ethan.

Robert (soft but firm)

"If there are, we handle it. Just like we trained."

Ethan nodded quickly, though his hands still trembled.

Robert (whispering, motioning ahead)

"I'll go first. Stay close."

Maya was next, then Ethan, and as quietly as possible, they descended into the dark.

The tunnel smelled of rot and damp earth. Every footstep echoed, bouncing off the curved walls.

Robert kept his flashlight low, moving carefully, listening. Every few steps, he stopped, ears tuned for any sound that wasn't theirs.

Maya walked just behind him, knife in hand, ready. Ethan followed last, small and silent, his breath shaky.

After a few minutes, the noise from the scavengers above faded.

They were safe. For now.

MAYA (whispering)

"How long until we're out?"

Robert glanced ahead. The tunnel stretched for at least another two hundred yards, ending at a broken grate on the far side of the highway. Beyond that was an old rest stop, which they could use as a place to regroup.

Robert (low voice)

"Not far. Just keep moving."

They walked in silence, the only sounds being the dripping of water from above and the occasional shuffle of rats in the debris.

Then Ethan froze.

Ethan (whispering, tense)

"Dad… I hear something."

Location: Midway through the Tunnel

Robert stopped instantly.

He turned off the flashlight, plunging them into pure blackness.

The three of them stood completely still.

And then they heard it.

A low shuffling sound farther ahead in the tunnel. Slow. Uneven.

A wet breath.

Maya's hand tightened around her knife.

Robert slowly unslung his rifle, keeping it close.

Whatever it was… it was alive.

For a long moment, the tunnel was deathly silent.

Then—

A shape moved in the darkness ahead.

A hunched figure dragging itself forward.

Robert raised his rifle, his finger just barely resting on the trigger.

Robert (low, commanding)

"Stop. Don't move."

The figure froze.

Maya breathed shallowly, her heart hammering.

Robert's eyes adjusted to the dark just enough to see what they were facing.

It was a man. Or at least, it had been.

His clothes tore, sores and burns covered his body, and his skin was pale and raw from radiation exposure. His eyes were hollow, sunken, lifeless, yet moving.

A wanderer. A dying man.

Ethan (whispers, scared)

"Is he… a bad guy?"

Robert didn't answer.

The man's mouth moved, barely making a sound. His lips cracked, and his throat was too dry to form words.

Then he staggered forward, reaching toward them with bony fingers.

Robert reacted instantly.

Robert (commanding, low voice)

"Back. Stay behind me."

Maya stepped back, gripping Ethan's arm, keeping him from moving closer.

The man groaned, stumbling forward another step, his fingers twitching like he was trying to speak.

Then, suddenly—

He collapsed.

The sound echoed, bouncing through the tunnel.

Silence.

Robert waited, watching.

The man didn't get up.

Maya exhaled slowly.

MAYA (whispering, relieved but shaken)

"He's… dead?"

Robert stepped forward cautiously, keeping his rifle ready.

The man was still breathing, but barely. His eyes twitched slightly, staring at nothing.

A dying survivor. Left behind. Forgotten.

There was nothing they could do for him.

Finally, Robert turned to his children.

Robert (low, quiet)

"We keep moving."

And they did.

In a Storm Drain Exit–Near the Old West Stop

The end of the tunnel finally came into view—a rusted metal grate, broken just enough for them to squeeze through.

Robert peeked outside first, checking the surroundings.

Beyond the storm drain was a cracked parking lot, overgrown with weeds. The old rest stop sat in the distance, its windows dark, its sign faded.

Someone abandoned it.

For now.

Robert (whispering, nodding)

"We're clear. Let's go."

One by one, they climbed out, stepping into the cool night air.

Maya stretched, shaking off the tension. Ethan just hugged himself, looking back toward the tunnel.

Ethan (softly, staring into the darkness)

"What if he wakes up?"

Robert glanced back. The dying man was still inside, his figure barely visible.

Robert didn't have an answer.

Instead, he gently placed a hand on Ethan's shoulder.

Robert (quiet, firm)

"Then we keep moving."

The three of them turned toward the rest stop, disappearing into the ruins of the world once more.

Emerging from the tunnel, Robert, Maya, and Ethan stepped cautiously into the dim afternoon light. The air outside was heavy with dust and the lingering scent of smoke, but it was a welcome change from the stale, suffocating air underground. Ahead of them, an abandoned rest stop sat eerily silent, its once-vibrant gas station sign flickering weakly against the overcast sky.

Robert took the lead, gripping his rifle as he approached the convenience store attached to the gas station. The parking lot was littered with rusting cars, some with doors left open, their interiors ransacked long ago. The group moved carefully, scanning their surroundings, their boots crunching softly on broken glass and scattered debris.

"Stay close," Robert murmured, glancing at his children. Maya nodded, already reaching for the pistol holstered at her hip. Ethan, still nervous but determined, stuck to his sister's side.

The shelves inside the store were empty, but Robert knew that desperate survivors often overlooked hidden caches. He gestured for Maya and Ethan to search while he checked behind the counter.

"Look for anything useful," he said.

Ethan rummaged through a toppled-over shelf, his small hands shifting through cans and wrappers. "What about this?" He held up a half-squashed granola bar.

Maya smirked. "We can do better."

They searched the aisles, looking for anything they might have missed. Maya found a first-aid kit behind the counter, while Robert pried open a locked cabinet and discovered a stash of bottled water. They were stuffing their bags when the sound of shuffling footsteps made them freeze.

"Easy there." A voice called from the entrance.

Robert spun around, gun raised, only to lower it slightly when he saw the man standing in the doorway. He was in his late thirties, lean with a rough beard, dressed in scavenged military gear. The rifle was in his hands, but he wasn't aiming it at them.

"I don't want trouble," the man said. "Just looking for supplies, like you."

Robert studied him, his eyes hard. "Who are you?"

"Paul," the man answered. He glanced at Maya and Ethan, then back to Robert. "You got kids… brave to bring them this far."

"We don't have a choice," Robert replied flatly.

Paul nodded in understanding. "No one does." He moved toward a nearby shelf, carefully pulling out a dented can of soup. "You headed anywhere specific?"

Robert hesitated, but Maya spoke up. "The city."

Paul's expression darkened. "Not a good idea."

"We don't care," Robert said. "We're looking for someone—my wife, their mother."

Paul sighed, setting the can down. "Look, I get it. I have a wife, too. But the city's a war zone. Resistance fighters and the Belvarian occupation forces are tearing it apart. The enemy had bombed the city a few weeks before. It won't be easy getting in, let alone finding someone."

Robert clenched his jaw. "Doesn't matter."

"I figured you'd say that." Paul exhaled, shaking his head. "Survivors like us don't get to have easy choices."

The distant sound of booms cut their conversation short, explosions rumbling through the air. A few seconds later, sporadic gunfire cracked through the city skyline.

Maya turned to Paul. "Is that—"

Paul grimaced. "Yeah. Fighting's getting worse."

Robert tensed, gripping his rifle tighter. He knew it was only a matter of time before the battle reached the outskirts.

Then, Maya stiffened. She saw movement—a figure sprinting toward them through the broken gas pumps. The invader, dressed in their uniform, swung his rifle across his chest and zeroed in on them.

Maya reacted before anyone else could. Her breath hitched, her fingers tightening around the pistol's grip. She lifted the weapon, steadied her aim, and pulled the trigger.

The shot rang out, echoing through the empty streets.

The soldier stumbled, a red mist bursting from his chest as he collapsed onto the cracked pavement.

For a moment, there was silence.

Maya stood frozen, her hands trembling slightly, the gun still aimed where the soldier had fallen.

Robert stepped toward her, placing a firm hand on her shoulder. His voice was steady, but there was a tightness to it. "You did what you had to do."

Maya swallowed hard and nodded, but she felt her stomach twist. She had taken a life.

Paul exhaled, impressed. "Not bad."

Robert looked down at his daughter, his pride battling against the ache in his chest. He had trained her to survive, to defend herself, but seeing her actually pull the trigger… it was different.

He squeezed her shoulder gently before stepping back. "Stay sharp. There might be more."

Maya steadied herself, inhaled deeply, and nodded. "I'm ready."

Paul glanced between them, then looked toward the city, where smoke was rising. "If you're serious about getting in, you're gonna need help."

Robert met his gaze. "You offering?"

Paul smirked grimly. "I've come this far alone. Might be nice to have some company."

Robert nodded. "Then let's move."

The four of them gathered their supplies, weapons in hand, and looked to the burning city.

They decided the city was the only way forward.

Paul had left to retrieve his wife, Harley, from a nearby safe house—a place he'd been using to lie low since escaping the resistance. He returned an hour later with her by his side. Harley was tough-looking, with auburn hair tied back in a messy ponytail, dirt smeared across her face, and a pistol holstered at her hip. She had a weary, hardened look of someone who had seen too much but still held on to hope.

"Jim says you're going in," she said, eyeing Robert, Maya, and Ethan. "You sure about this?"

Robert nodded. "We're sure."

"Then we'd better be smart about it," Paul said, pulling out a crumpled map. "The main roads are suicide—completely locked down by Belvarian occupation forces, checkpoints, and sniper nests. But there's a weak spot." He pointed to the south side of the city. "There's an open gate here. It's risky—minimal cover, and if we get spotted, we're sitting ducks. But if we move fast and stick together, we can make it."

Robert traced the map with his finger. "That's our way in."

Paul nodded. "Before we move, I have something for you two." He led them to an overturned supply crate near the gas station. Inside, he pulled out two sets of body armor—scarred and worn, but still intact. "Standard resistance gear. It won't stop a sniper round, but it'll keep you from getting shredded by shrapnel."

Maya hesitated before taking hers. "Feels… heavy."

"You get used to it," Paul said.

He reached back into the crate and handed Robert and Maya upgraded rifles—sleek, well-maintained, fitted with holographic sights. "These will serve you better than what you've been carrying."

Robert inspected his new weapon and nodded in approval. "Appreciate it."

With their weapons loaded and their gear secured, they prepared to move.

Ethan swallowed hard. "Are you sure this is the best way?"

Robert knelt beside his son. "There is no best way, buddy. But it's the only way to find Mom."

Ethan nodded, gripping his small backpack tighter. He was afraid, but he trusted his father.

Into the Fire

Under the cover of night, they ran.

The war-torn city loomed ahead—towers of shattered glass and steel, roads choked with debris, smoke rising from distant fires. Explosions lit up the skyline like a dying heartbeat, and the distant echoes of gunfire and screaming filled the air.

Paul led them through the cracked pavement of the industrial district, ducking between ruined buildings. The stench of death and burning metal made Maya's stomach turn.

"Keep moving," Robert whispered.

As they neared the south gate, they spotted the real danger—drones.

Three of them hovered above, scanning the ruins with bright red sensors, sweeping back and forth in eerie synchronization. Below them, mechanical dogs patrolled the streets, their gun-mounted bodies moving with unnatural precision.

Maya's breath caught in her throat. "What the hell are those?"

"Security drones. Automated tracking units," Paul muttered. "They'll flag us in seconds if we're out in the open."

Harley scanned the area. "We need a distraction."

Paul nodded. "I can make something work. You all get into that building on the right. When the moment comes, you run for the next cover."

Robert hesitated. "You sure about this?"

"Trust me."

Without another word, Paul pulled a small EMP grenade from his vest. He signaled to Robert to go, then sprinted in the opposite direction.

Robert, Maya, Ethan, and Harley rushed into the abandoned structure—a collapsed parking garage, its floors cracked and uneven. They crouched behind a concrete barrier, peeking out.

Paul raised his arm, activated the EMP, and tossed it.

Though silent, the explosion's effect was immediate. The hovering drones flickered, their red eyes dimming. The robotic dogs stumbled, their weapons lowering.

"Now!" Paul shouted.

Robert grabbed Ethan and ran. Maya followed, her heart hammering.

The city swallowed them whole.

The tension was suffocating.

Robert's jaw was tight, his fingers flexing over his rifle as they ducked inside the ruins of an old office building. Dust and debris coated the cracked floors, shattering glass, crunching beneath their boots.

Paul sat against the wall, catching his breath. His wife, Harley, pressed a torn cloth against the graze on her arm, wincing as she applied pressure. Ethan watched with wide eyes but said nothing. Maya, rifle in hand, kept her gaze on her father and Paul, sensing the rising tension.

"Are you trying to get my family killed?" Robert snapped, stepping closer to Paul. His voice was low but sharp.

Paul held up a hand. "Calm down. I wouldn't play games like that. My wife is here too."

Robert exhaled through gritted teeth, trying to rein in his frustration. "Now they know we're here. They're searching in numbers."

Paul's expression didn't change. "We knew this was gonna be dangerous. Getting spotted was a risk from the start."

Harley finished patching herself up and looked at them. "He's right. We don't have time to argue."

Robert sighed, forcing his anger down. "This is gonna be stressful."

"Then focus," Paul said firmly. "Transfer that anger where it belongs—toward the occupational forces."

Maya watched the exchange closely. She had never seen her father that rattled before. She understood, though—he was carrying all of their survival on his shoulders.

They didn't have time to dwell.

The Hunt Begins

From outside, they could hear the occupational forces moving. Heavy boots pounded against pavement, voices barking orders in clipped, foreign tones. A squad was searching the area, sweeping through the buildings one by one.

"They're coming in formation," Harley whispered, peeking through a crack in the wall. "Looks like a full search team."

Robert cursed under his breath.

"Up the stairs," Paul suggested. "Higher ground gives us an advantage."

Robert didn't like it, but they didn't have a better option.

They moved fast, keeping low as they ascended the cracked stairwell. Maya could hear the soldiers below—rifles clicking, boots shifting over broken glass. They were close.

Then—

Bang! Bang!

Gunfire erupted below as one soldier spotted movement. A sharp whistle of bullets cut through the air as the squad opened fire.

"Move!" Robert shouted.

They sprinted up the last flight of stairs, bullets biting into the walls behind them, sending chunks of concrete flying.

Harley stumbled, a bullet grazing her leg. She hissed in pain but kept running.

Maya turned and fired down the stairwell, forcing the soldiers to duck for cover. Paul did the same, his shots controlled and precise.

They reached the top floor—an exposed office level with broken windows, giving them a view of the war-torn city stretching beneath them. Smoke curled in the distance, and the sounds of distant fighting echoed from all directions.

Paul pulled Maya behind cover, breathing hard. "We're in the middle of their AO now."

Robert turned, scanning their surroundings. "We need to move before they pin us down."

Then, in the distance—

A glint.

Maya barely had time to react before—

BOOM!

A bullet ripped through the air, striking the concrete next to them with a deafening impact.

"Sniper!" Paul yelled.

They scrambled for cover as another shot rang out, blasting a massive hole into the floor where they had just stood.

This wasn't just any sniper—this was an elite.

Their most dangerous enemy yet had locked onto them.

The Hunter and the Hunted

The next shot came like lightning.

BOOM!

A crater exploded in the concrete near Ethan's feet, sending dust and shrapnel flying. He yelped as Robert yanked him down behind a collapsed desk.

"Stay low!" Robert barked.

They had a second to react. The sniper wasn't just skilled—he was fast, repositioning after each shot to keep them guessing.

Paul swore under his breath as he crouched behind a thick steel filing cabinet. "This isn't some random marksman. That's an elite."

Harley pressed against a shattered window frame, wincing from her wound. "Makes sense. They don't send their best unless we're really pissing them off."

Maya, heart hammering, peeked around a piece of rubble. About 200 yards away, a sniper had positioned themselves on the skeleton of a half-destroyed high-rise. From here, he was nothing more than a dark figure hidden in the jagged shadows.

"We have no angle," Robert muttered, scanning their surroundings. "If we move, he'll pick us off."

Paul exhaled sharply. "We can't stay pinned down. We need to flush him out."

"Easier said than done," Harley grunted.

Maya's hands tightened on her rifle. Her father was right. Move and die. Stay and die. They needed to change the rules of the game.

A thought struck her.

She turned to Paul. "You said they have drones up, right?"

Paul nodded. "Yeah, but what's your—"

"Then he's probably using them to track us," Maya said. "Which means he's not just watching the windows. He's watching the sky."

Robert's eyes narrowed, following her train of thought. "You're saying… we use that against him."

Maya nodded.

Paul smirked. "Smart. But we'll need a distraction."

Robert exhaled. "I'll do it."

Maya's breath caught. "Dad—"

"I'm the best shot here," Robert said firmly. "Paul, you and Maya set up for a counterstrike. Harley, cover Ethan. I'll bait the bastard."

Paul hesitated, then gave a sharp nod. "Alright. Just don't die, old man."

Robert gave his daughter a look. "Maya, when I move, you watch him. The moment you see an opening, you take it. You understand me?"

Maya swallowed hard but nodded. "I got it."

Ethan clutched his dad's arm. "Be careful."

Robert gave him a reassuring squeeze. "Always."

The Decoy

With a deep breath, Robert steeled himself.

Then—

He ran.

Instantly, the sniper fired.

BOOM!

A round obliterated the desk he had been crouching behind just moments ago. Robert rolled to the side, zigzagging across the open floor, forcing the sniper to track him.

Maya's eyes locked onto the sniper's position.

There.

The sniper shifted momentarily, exposed. A slight movement of his gun barrel as he adjusted for another shot.

This was her moment.

Maya breathed.

Time slowed.

She focused—hands steady, lining up the shot.

The sniper's head shifted, angling toward her father.

Maya squeezed the trigger.

CRACK!

Her bullet whipped through the air.

A split second later—

A spray of red mist burst from the high-rise as the sniper's body jerked violently backward.

Silence.

Maya didn't move. She didn't breathe.

Then—

Paul let out a whoop. "Hell yeah! That's how you do it!"

Harley exhaled a breath of relief.

Robert, crouched behind a broken pillar, turned toward Maya. His face was unreadable for a moment. Then—he smiled.

"That was a perfect shot," he said, pride clear in his voice.

Maya let out a shaky breath, lowering her rifle. "I—I got him."

"You saved us," Ethan whispered in awe.

Paul clapped a hand on her shoulder. "Took out a damn elite. You're one of us now."

Maya's heart was still pounding, but she met her father's gaze.

Robert gave her a slow nod. "Good work."

She nodded back.

But there was no time to celebrate.

In the distance, the sounds of approaching vehicles and heavy boots filled the air. The occupational forces hadn't finished yet.

Robert stood, reloading his weapon. "Let's move. We still have a city to cross."

And with that, they pressed forward—deeper into the war-torn city, the fire of determination burning stronger than ever.

CHAPTER 4

SHE GOT THE JOB

The city's heart was in ruins.

Robert, Maya, Ethan, Paul, and Harley moved through the crumbling streets, the acrid smell of smoke and decay thick in the air. The once-thriving metropolis had become a graveyard—skeletal buildings stood like broken tombstones, their charred remains whispering the stories of the lives that had once filled them.

Then they saw it.

The building where she had been.

Shattered windows and warped beams showed the structure was only a burnt-out husk, towering over us. The floors had collapsed in sections, leaving jagged edges exposed like the ribs of a long-dead beast. The remnants of a missile strike had caved in the center of the building, leaving a gaping hole surrounded by blackened debris.

Maya's breath hitched. Ethan froze, his small hands trembling. Robert's knees nearly gave out.

This was it.

This was where she had been last.

Robert staggered forward, pressing his palm against the scorched remains of the front desk. He could still picture her there—smiling, holding her resume, excited for the future.

Maya fell to her knees, sobs wracking her body. Ethan clutched his sister's arm, rocking his head.

"No," he choked out. "No, no, no! Mom, please!"

Robert dropped his rifle and pulled his children into his arms, gripping them as if holding them tighter would make the moment less real. His throat burned, and tears blurred his vision.

"I love you, baby," he whispered, voice breaking. He buried his face in Maya's hair, clutching Ethan just as fiercely.

"I'm sorry I couldn't protect you."

A deep, soul-wrenching pain clawed at his chest. He had kept moving, kept fighting, because in his heart, he had clung to the hope that he'd find her alive. But now, standing here, the weight of reality crushed him.

"I promise I'll take care of them," he whispered. "Until my last breath. You'd be so proud of them. So proud."

Paul and Harley stood at a respectful distance, their faces wet with tears. They had seen loss, had lived it, but nothing could prepare someone for a moment like this.

Then Ethan gasped.

A pile of bodies lay nearby, some half-buried in rubble.

Maya's stomach turned, bile rising in her throat.

"No," she whispered.

Robert's hands shook as he forced himself to move. They had to know.

One by one, they checked the faces of the fallen, their hands numb, their chests tightening with every glimpse of someone who wasn't here.

Then Maya saw it.

A wedding ring.

Her mother's wedding ring.

She reached out with trembling fingers, brushing away the dust and grime. Beside the ring was a delicate silver necklace—her mother's, unmistakably hers.

Maya wiped them clean, pressing them to her chest.

Robert's hands clenched into fists.

Ethan swallowed hard. "She's… not here," he said.

A brief flicker of relief cut through the anguish.

"She's not here," Maya repeated, a desperate hope creeping into her voice. "Maybe she—maybe she got away?"

Robert slowly took the ring and slipped it into his pocket, his grief still raw, but a small part of him wanting to believe. Maya carefully put the necklace around her neck, feeling the weight settle against her heart.

"She was here," Robert whispered. "But… she's gone now."

"Maybe they moved the bodies," Maya murmured, though she wasn't sure if she was trying to convince Ethan or herself.

Ethan sniffled, wiping his face. "Maybe we didn't find her because… because she's not here." His voice was shaky, but there was something else there—something stubborn.

Maya turned to him, her heart aching. "Ethan—"

"No, listen," he said, his small hands balling into fists. "What if she's alive? What if she escaped? What if—"

Maya swallowed, pulling him into a hug.

"Ethan," she whispered, her voice thick with emotion. "We have to think about ourselves now. We have to honor Mom's memory."

He sniffled against her shoulder. "Okay… but I'm not ready to stop believing yet."

She smiled sadly, holding him tighter. "I understand."

A Flicker of Light

Maya wiped her tears and turned back toward the wreckage. Her mother had been interviewing here. What if something remained?

She sprinted toward the gaping hole where the missile had struck, clambering over fallen concrete and steel.

"Maya!" Robert called, but she didn't stop.

She reached a half-buried metal filing cabinet, its edges blackened but still intact. She pried it open, digging through the scorched papers inside.

Her heart pounded as she flipped through the burnt memos, half-melted ID cards, interview forms—

And then, she found it.

Her mother's file.

Maya's breath caught in her throat.

She tore through the pages, her fingers shaking. And then there it was.

A job offer.

Her mother had gotten the job.

Maya's grief cracked, replaced with something else joy.

She let out a half-laugh, half-sob, holding up the paper like it was the most precious thing in the world.

"She got the job!" she screamed, her voice raw. "Dad! Ethan! She got the job!"

Robert and Ethan rushed to her side, looking at the paper with wide eyes.

A smile broke across Robert's tear-streaked face. He nodded, blinking back more tears.

"She got it," he whispered.

Maya carefully tucked the papers into her jacket. It wasn't much, but it was something.

Paul and Harley stood nearby, quietly wiping their faces.

Harley took Paul's hand, squeezing it. "They still have each other," she whispered.

Paul swallowed hard. "We all do."

The Road Ahead

As the sun set behind the ruined city, the group stood together, weary but alive.

The war wasn't over. The journey wasn't done.

But they had made it this far.

Robert clutched his children close, his voice quiet but steady.

"We keep moving." "Let's get out of this Tier 4 Suppression Zone."

And so they did—walking forward, carrying their love, their grief, and their hope into the unknown.

CHAPTER 5

TAKE A BREATH

The moment of peace was short-lived.

Shouts erupted from the streets, followed by the sharp crack of gunfire.

Robert instinctively pulled Ethan behind cover while Maya snapped her rifle up, eyes scanning the incoming threat.

A squad of occupational soldiers had spotted them.

"Go!" Paul shouted, shouldering his weapon. "We'll hold them off!"

Harley was already moving, taking cover behind a toppled concrete barrier and returning fire.

Robert hesitated—he hated running from a fight.

But then he saw Paul glance back at him, giving a knowing nod.

They both understood.

Paul and Harley weren't just fighting to buy time. They were staying behind.

Robert clenched his jaw, emotions warring inside him. He hated to leave them. But he had Maya. He had Ethan.

And they deserved to live.

Robert gave Paul a firm nod, a silent thank you.

Then, gripping his children's hands, he ran.

As they sprinted through the ruined streets, gunfire echoed behind them. Paul and Harley kept firing, drawing the soldiers' attention away.

Maya looked back once, watching them disappear into the chaos.

"They'll be okay," she whispered, though she wasn't sure if she believed it.

Robert kept his focus forward. "We will remember them."

Reaching the Resistance

Minutes stretched into eternity as they ran through the war-torn city. Explosions thumped in the distance, and the air was thick with smoke. Every corner they turned could have led to more soldiers, another battle, another tragedy.

But then—

A barricade.

And beyond it, armed figures in makeshift uniforms.

Resistance fighters.

Robert raised his hands, keeping his rifle low but visible. "We're not hostile!"

The resistance soldiers snapped their weapons up, eyes narrowing.

One of them stepped forward, a hardened woman with a scar running across her cheek. "Who are you?"

Robert exhaled, his body nearly giving out. "We're survivors."

The woman studied them for a moment, then signaled her men to stand down.

"Bring them in," she ordered.

Finally. Finally, they were safe.

A flicker of hope lit in the hearts of the family.

The resistance base was a repurposed underground parking structure, reinforced with barricades and manned with guards. Inside, dozens of survivors gathered, eating, resting, sharing stories of what they had lost.

Someone provided Robert and his kids with authentic food. Warm, filling.

Maya ate in silence, the weight of their journey still pressing on her.

Ethan, however, was restless. He kept looking at the surrounding people, as if searching for something.

Or someone.

Then, as Robert explained everything they had endured since the nuke fell, a resistance fighter spoke up.

"A woman matching that description came through here a few weeks ago."

Maya's spoon clattered against the table. Robert's heart stopped.

Ethan's eyes lit up. "I told you!" He practically jumped from his seat, looking at his sister with an excited grin.

Maya blinked, her mind racing. "You're sure?"

The fighter nodded. "Red hair, determined look, wouldn't stop asking about survivors heading this way."

Robert clenched his fists. She made it this far.

Hope flared in his chest—raw, powerful, dangerous.

Ethan beamed, turning to Maya. "Maybe?"

Maya bit her lip, emotions swirling in her eyes. Then finally, she allowed herself a small, trembling smile.

"Maybe."

For the first time in a long time, the road ahead wasn't just about survival.

It was about finding her.

And they wouldn't stop until they did.

With the Belvarian Occupation forces declaring Robert, Maya, Ethan, and Robert's wife as Target 1 priorities, their journey becomes infinitely more dangerous. The occupation forces posted bounties in every occupied town, marking them as high-value fugitives. Wanted posters with their descriptions spread rapidly, making it nearly impossible to blend in.

Robert, now fully aware of the relentless pursuit, changes their tactics. He insists on traveling at night, avoiding main roads, and using disguises when necessary. He and Maya scout ahead, calculating every move. Ethan, though still young, learns quickly—adapting to life as a fugitive, keeping his head down, and following orders without hesitation.

As they push forward, they encounter bounty hunters—not just Belvarian Occupation soldiers, but mercenaries and desperate survivors willing to turn them in for food and resources. One night, while passing through an abandoned gas station, Maya spots a group of armed men whispering near a bounty poster. She overhears them planning an ambush at a nearby crossroads. Knowing they're being hunted, they change course immediately.

Their journey takes them into the deep wilderness, a rugged terrain where radiation-mutated wildlife is just as deadly as the soldiers hunting them. A brutal encounter with a mutated bear leaves Robert injured, forcing Maya to take the lead. She and Ethan work together to treat his wounds and keep him moving, proving that they're no longer just children—they're survivors.

Someone also marked Robert's wife as Target 1 priority threat to the occupation. As a resistance leader, she finds herself in increasing danger, with spies and informants tracking her every move. When she learns about the bounties, a chilling realization sets in: her husband and children are alive—but now, every enemy knows it too.

Despite the overwhelming odds, the family continues its desperate march toward the rumored resistance stronghold. But with every town locked down and every passing stranger a potential threat, the question remains: can they reach safety before they're caught?

Robert, Maya, and Ethan encountered an eerie silence as they entered the new city. Unlike the wastelands they've trudged through, this place is seemingly untouched by the war—no crumbling buildings, no fires, no signs of destruction. The streets are clean, and the skyscrapers still stand tall, casting long shadows over the empty roads.

But there are no people. No signs of life, no bodies, no bloodstains—just emptiness.

Maya grips her rifle tightly, scanning the buildings. "This isn't right," she mutters. Robert agrees. They discovered that the Belvarian occupation forces had destroyed or were swarming every other city they encountered, but they saw nothing here. It feels like a ghost town, but not in the way war-torn cities do. This place feels preserved.

Ethan, though cautious, is in awe. "It looks like people just… vanished," he whispers.

As they explore deeper, they find fully stocked stores, untouched apartments with clothes still folded, and even half-eaten meals left on dining tables, long since spoiled. Whatever happened here—it was sudden.

Then they notice the odd details. No wildlife, not even birds or rats. Dust did not collect over time, as if the city had frozen in time. No graffiti or signs of looting—a rarity in this lawless world.

And then, they find the first real clue. A newspaper sitting on a cafe counter, untouched by the elements. The date is from the exact day the war started.

That's when Robert realizes—this city wasn't just abandoned. The city was abandoned all at once.

Then, Ethan notices something even stranger. A single streetlight still flickered in the distance. Someone—or something—is still here.

As they cautiously follow the flickering streetlight's glow, a raspy voice echoes through the empty city streets.

"Who's there?"

Robert, Maya, and Ethan freeze, gripping their weapons. The voice is strained, like someone who hasn't spoken to another soul in years.

"Who are you?" the voice calls again, this time from the shadows of a crumbling bookstore. A frail figure steps into view, wrapped in tattered clothing, his beard long and unkempt. His eyes are wide, darting between them with both fear and curiosity.

Robert steps forward, keeping his hands visible. "We're just passing through," he says. "We mean no harm."

The man squints at them, studying their faces. He seems unsure, almost paranoid, but then he sighs and mutters, "If you were with them, you wouldn't be talking. You'd have already shot me."

This catches Robert's attention. "Them?"

The man hesitates, then waves them inside the bookstore. "Come in. If you're real, I don't want to be talking out here."

Inside, the store is dusty but strangely well-preserved, as if someone has been keeping it in order. The old man lights a lantern and sits in a chair that someone has used a thousand times.

"I thought I was the last one," he muttered, rubbing his forehead. "No one's been here in… God knows how long."

Maya looks around. "What happened to this place?"

The man chuckles dryly. "That's the million-dollar question, isn't it? One day, everyone was here. The next… they weren't. No bombs. No bodies. Just gone."

Ethan frowns. "But… where did they go?"

The man shakes his head. "I don't know. But I stayed. I saw the warnings—got ready to run like everyone else. But something told me not to. Maybe I was crazy. Maybe I still am. But I swear…" He leans in, lowering his voice. "They left because something worse was coming."

Robert, Maya, and Ethan exchange uneasy glances.

The man sits back, observing them. "So tell me… why are you here? And what are you running from?"

The old man sighs, rubbing his temples as if reliving the past. "They left because the city was supposed to be nuked."

Robert narrows his eyes. "Supposed to be?"

The man nods. "Yeah. The sirens blared; the warnings came through. Authorities ordered evacuations, and people ran like hell. But then… nothing. No bombs. No air raids. Just silence."

Maya frowns. "Why?"

He lets out a dry chuckle. "Turns out, this city wasn't 'strategically important enough.' Not worth wasting a warhead on. The Belvarian occupation forces and the invading armies focused on the bigger targets. But by the time the higher-ups realized that, it was too late. Everyone had already left, thinking they had minutes to live."

Ethan shivers. "So… they abandoned it for nothing?"

The man nods. "Exactly. An entire city emptied in a single day. And since it never got hit, no one ever came back. No military, no refugees, no scavengers. Just me." He waves his hands around the dusty bookstore. "And the ghosts."

Maya crosses her arms. "You don't actually believe there are ghosts here, do you?"

The old man's expression darkens. "Not ghosts, the way you're thinking. But something is off about this place." He glances toward the boarded-up windows. "You ever notice how quiet it is? No birds, no rats, not even the wind. It's like the city itself is… waiting."

Robert exchanges a glance with Maya and Ethan. The city's eerie stillness had unsettled them the moment they arrived, and now, knowing its history, it felt even stranger.

The old man leans forward. "So tell me, what the hell are you three doing here? Nobody comes here."

Robert takes a deep breath. "We're on the run. The Belvarian occupation forces put bounties on us. We needed somewhere to rest, somewhere quiet."

The man whistles low. "Well, you sure found quiet. But if you're on the run, this place might be both the safest and most dangerous place for you. No one's looking for you here… but if they do come, they'll notice real quick that someone's been stirring up dust."

Maya exhales sharply. "So, what do we do?"

The old man shrugs. "That depends. Are you just passing through? Or are you looking for something more?"

Reluctantly, Robert and Maya come clean. They tell the old man about their desperate search for Robert's wife—Maya's mother—the only thing keeping them moving forward. They recount the chaos of the war, the nuclear strikes, the occupation, and how they've been fighting to survive ever since. As the words leave their mouths, a creeping doubt settles in.

Maybe they're being foolish. Maybe this mission is impossible. Maybe they're just chasing ghosts in a world that has already taken too much from them.

The old man listens, his lined face unreadable. Then, after a long silence, he exhales sharply and leans back.

"Well, hell," he mutters. "You're not crazy. Or maybe you are, but if you are, then so am I."

Robert and Maya exchange a look. "What do you mean?" Robert asks.

The old man scratches his scruffy beard, eyes flickering with something unreadable. "I know her," he says simply. "Your wife. She's the only woman I've seen in a long time."

Maya's breath catches. Robert stiffens.

"She was here?" Maya asks, her voice barely above a whisper.

The man nods. "Recently. A few weeks, maybe. She passed through, just like you. Didn't stay long, but she was alive." He shakes his head, almost laughing at the absurdity of it. "Guess the world ain't done playing with you folks yet."

Robert grips the edge of the table, his knuckles turning white. For the first time in a long time, a fragile ember of hope flickers in his chest.

"Where did she go?" he asks, voice tight with urgency.

The old man sighs. "She was heading west, same as you. Toward the mountains. Toward the resistance." He studies Robert and Maya carefully. "If you're serious about finding her… that's where you need to go."

Maya swallows hard, her heart pounding. After everything, after all the suffering, the near-misses, and the doubt…

They are finally on her trail.

The old man exhales, rubbing his face. "So what do you want? Just passing through? Or are you looking for something more?"

Robert hesitates, then finally admits reluctantly, "We need rest."

The man chuckles, shaking his head. "Figured as much." He gestures around the abandoned bookstore. "Well, you won't find a five-star hotel, but you're welcome to stay—for a little while."

Maya narrows her eyes. "Why help us?"

The man sighs, looking out the window at the empty streets. "Because I've been alone too long. And because… maybe it's nice to feel useful again."

He stands up, cracking his stiff joints. "But let's get one thing straight. This place may be quiet, but that doesn't mean it's safe. You stay too long, and the wrong eyes are gonna notice."

Robert clenches his jaw, reluctantly nodding. "We just need a little time. Then we'll move."

The old man studies him for a long moment, then sighs. "Alright, then. Follow me. I'll show you where you can sleep."

As they move deeper into the bookstore, Ethan glances up at Robert and whispers, "Are we really safe here?"

Robert doesn't answer right away. His eyes scan the darkened shelves, the dust settling around them, the eerie silence pressing in. Reluctantly, he murmurs, "For now."

Toward them, she might walk straight into danger.

For the first time in a long while, the tension eases. As the night settles over the abandoned city, the group finds a rare moment of peace.

Ethan, wide-eyed with excitement, discovers an old arcade machine in the back of the bookstore, miraculously still functional thanks to a backup generator the old man had rigged. He laughs, forgetting the weight of survival, his fingers tapping the controls as he loses himself in a game he hadn't played in years.

Maya, flipping through the pages of a book she found on a dusty shelf, sighs with contentment. She's almost forgotten what it feels like to read something that isn't a survival manual or a map. For just a little while, she isn't a fugitive, a fighter—just a girl getting lost in a story.

Robert, meanwhile, sits across from the old man at a makeshift table made of stacked books, sharing a meal. They chat about life before the war, trading stories of the past. The old man talks about how he used to run a record shop, how people used to come from miles around to browse vinyl, how music made the world feel alive. Robert tells him about his family, about how Maya is too stubborn for her own good, and how Ethan used to fear thunderstorms. The conversation flows easily, and they chuckle as if they aren't on the run for one night.

It's a brief escape, but it means everything.

Yet, beyond the city, danger still looms. Unbeknownst to them, the resistance out west is not what it used to be. Their leader, a man of principle and strategy, died long ago, and in his place, the resistance has grown desperate, paranoid, and ruthless. They see everyone as a potential threat, including Robert's wife, who is heading straight for them, thinking she'll find allies.

Robert, Maya, and Ethan don't know it yet, but the moment they set out again, their journey will become even more dangerous. And by the time they realize the truth... it may already be too late.

The resistance leader's stern gaze met Robert's. "Information isn't free," he said. "If you want our help, you need to help us first."

They agreed to gather supplies and intel. The mission was straightforward, but during their scavenging, an ambush turned it into chaos. Bullets whizzed by as they barely escaped, realizing the enemy was closer than they thought.

Meanwhile, the story shifts to the Belvarian occupation forces' camp. Their leader, General Bronn, revealed their motive: a deep-seated grudge against the country for past conflicts and resource control. They believed that using nukes would cripple the nation, making it easier to conquer. Bronn's cold eyes reflected a relentless hatred and a hunger for power.

Back with Robert and his children, the stakes were higher than ever. Armed with new information and a deeper understanding of their enemy, they prepared for the next steps in their perilous journey.

After receiving the news about her mother's whereabouts, Maya's heart surged with hope. Yet, exhaustion from the long journey, hunger, and thirst overwhelmed her. She felt dizzy, and then everything went black.

In that moment of unconsciousness, her mind took her back to a warm memory: her mother cooking breakfast, the aroma filling the air, her brother's playful teasing before school. It was a vivid, comforting scene, a stark contrast to her present reality. This memory reminded her of what she was fighting for, even as she lay unconscious.

His whispered prayer hung in the air, a quiet plea for a miracle. With renewed hope and strength, Robert and his children set off once more, determined to reunite their family against all odds.

CHAPTER 6

THE BITTER MARCH

"The air cut sharper than any blade, its icy tendrils creeping into every crevice. As Robert, Maya, and Ethan moved through the icy wasteland, the world around them lay frozen in a silent, deadly embrace. Each step was a testament to their will to survive in a season where death waited at every corner." The temperature dropped 40 degrees below normal winter temperatures. At a chilling -25 degrees, everything for miles—metal, blood, and sound. Even the wind stopped screaming. It whispered now, dragging ash and ice across a dead world. Maya coughed as she tightened her scarf across her face. "I thought the war was the worst thing we'd have to deal with; I never thought the weather could be this bad. Ethan and Robert silently agreed, too cold to speak, and they trudged on through the 3-foot-thick and rough snow that could cut like glass. The cold bit at their legs, fingers, and face—merciless, hungry. It didn't care who they were or what they had already survived. It just wanted to wear them down. The snow was coming down sideways now — thick, fast, and blinding. A full whiteout. The blizzard that didn't just cover the ground but swallowed it. "I think I see a cabin," Maya mumbled, then crawled inside the cabin. Robert shut the door and sighed, "Thank God! We have a home again!" Ethan exclaimed. They all collapsed, sleeping next to each other for 24 hours. "We need to look around to see if you can find anything like food or supplies, and watch out for mutants. Robert ordered, "Don't say that, Dad. I'll be too scared to go into the basement," Maya joked slightly seriously. "Yeah, Dad is not cool," Ethan echoed. Maya and Ethan

The cold bit into their skin as Maya, Ethan, and Robert trudged through the snow-covered landscape. The cabin they'd found had offered minimal respite, and the blizzard outside made it clear they needed a more permanent solution. As they descended into a hidden underground passage, warmth enveloped them, a welcome change from the brutal weather above.

A figure approached, cloaked in layers that hinted at both practicality and ritual. "Welcome, travelers," he said, his voice echoing off the stone walls. "You've found sanctuary from the storm."

They were led deeper into the subterranean enclave, where the air grew warmer and the space opened into a bustling community. People moved about with purpose, offering nods and smiles as the newcomers passed. It all seemed almost too perfect.

As they settled in, a sense of unease crept in. Subtle symbols adorned the walls, and whispered conversations hinted at a deeper layer to this society. One evening, their host approached them with a serene smile. "We honor the ancient ones here," he explained, gesturing around. "And we expect all within our walls to do the same."

Maya exchanged a glance with Ethan and Robert. They knew then that their stay here would be anything but simple.

Maya, Ethan, and Robert trudge through knee-deep snow, their breath visible in the frigid air. The sound of distant engines fades as they find shelter in a dense thicket.

ETHAN:

"Do you think we lost them?"

ROBERT:

"Let's hope. Keep moving."

They push forward, spotting a hidden entrance to an underground bunker. They slip inside, closing the hatch behind them.

They find themselves in a makeshift underground city. Warm lights flicker, and the air smells of cooking food. Kind faces greet them.

ELDER:

"Welcome, travelers. You look cold and weary. Come, share a meal with us."

They follow the elder to a communal area, where a pot of stew bubbles. They eat, but Maya and Ethan exchange wary glances.

MAYA: (whispering)

"Something's off."

Ethan: (nodding)

"Yeah. These people are too… reverent."

Before they can discuss further, a bell chimes. The people around them bow deeply. The elder gestures for them to do the same.

ELDER:

"At midnight, we honor our leader. Please join us."

Robert: (calmly)

"We'll observe. Thank you."

The elder smiles, but there's a hint of disappointment. After the ritual, they're led to a small hut. Inside, a man awaits them.

MAN: (hushed)

"I saw you refuse. You're not alone. Some of us want out. This place isn't what it seems."

He explains the cult's grip, the forced reverence, and their desire to escape.

MAYA:

"We'll help you. But we need a plan."

The man nods, determination in his eyes. He had taken the first step toward freedom.

The cult leader's second-in-command nervously approaches.

SECOND:

"They've disobeyed again. We should take them out."

CULT LEADER: (calmly)

"That won't be necessary. They will come around."

The cult gathers again, performing another odd ritual. Maya and Ethan refuse to take part.

MAYA:

"This is madness. We won't bow to your leader."

The room falls silent, shocked by the defiance. The second glares at them.

SECOND:

"I told you! They need to be dealt with!"

The cult leader executes his second in cold blood, blaming him for the ruckus. Fearing head loses grip on his power.

A firefight erupts as Maya, Ethan, and Robert fend off the cultists, escaping back to the alley's hut.

ALLY: (urgent whisper)

"Now's our chance. We've rigged a bomb to cover our escape."

They race through the underground city, the firefight intensifying. The bomb detonated, collapsing the bunker and giving them the cover they needed to escape into the frosty night. The family met at Allies Hut.

Maya, Ethan, and Robert sit with the two former cult members, a man and a woman, who look relieved but wary.

MAYA:

"How did it come to this?"

MAN: (sighing)

"We were just ordinary people. When the nuclear invasion hit, we fled to the bunker. We never imagined it would turn out like this."

WOMAN:

"We came from a city that's now a ghost town. It was normal at first. He was a good leader, but the power went to his head."

ETHAN:

"And people just went along with it?"

MAN:

"People needed hope. Food, shelter… It was easier to believe he was some savior. But now, he's no different than the dictators who attacked our country."

Maya and Josh, former cult members, thanked Maya and her family for saving them. Maya "were just trying to survive, but you're welcome, I'm glad we could help." "Robert, there's something you need to know. We're being hunted by the Belvarian occupation forces. It won't be safe following us; you could die," Maya and Josh said. "We are really ready to take that risk, Robert." After a few weeks, they found a new place to stay in an abandoned building. They found shelter in what used to be a hardware store—dusty, with cracked windows, and shelves still lined with rusted tools. Maya leaned against the wall, breathing heavy. "We're actually out," she whispered. "I can't believe it." As Maya, Ethan, Robert, and Josh shared a quick meal under the fading spring sun, there was a rare sense of calm. They huddled close around the fire, the warmth brushing their faces as dusk settled in. The air smelled faintly of dew and smoke—spring had brought new life, even to a dying world.

Josh leaned back, a soft grin tugging at his face. "I used to go fishing with my grandfather," he said. "He'd wake me up before dawn, and we'd sit by this tiny lake, half-asleep, barely talking. But those mornings stuck with me."

Robert looked up, eyes distant. "I used to fish," he whispered. "Back before all this. Taught my kids, too. You learn patience out there… and how to sit with silence."

Josh nodded. "Yeah… that's the part I miss most."

Maya took a bite of canned beans and smiled gently. "We used to plant a garden. My mom and I. Every year, we'd grow these tiny red flowers by the windowsill. I didn't know it back then, but I think it was her way of keeping hope alive."

Maya's face softened. "My mom used to hum when she worked in the kitchen. Same tune, every time. I can't remember the name, but… I still hear it sometimes. In my head."

Silence settled over the group—not heavy, but warm. Shared memories. Shared loss. For once, they weren't just survivors. They were people holding onto slivers of who they used to be.

But before the moment could settle, a low hum pierced the silence. The sound of boots. Drones. Metal scraping against pavement.

Robert didn't hesitate. "Move. Now."

The first shot came through the window like thunder.

The crack of gunfire split the air before anyone could speak. Maya dropped instantly, her body twisting mid-step. Josh barely turned before a second round caught him in the chest. No warning. No time to scream.

"Maya, down!" Robert shouted, yanking her behind a broken counter as glass exploded around them. Ethan dove beside her, breathing hard, his face pale.

The silence that followed was cruel—just the whir of a passing drone and the echo of death hanging in the dust.

Before they could run, Ethan and Maya froze. Maya and Josh lay still—eyes wide, blood soaking into the cracked tile. They'd seen death before. Too many times. But this… this felt different. These two had shared laughter, stories, and even hope. It was starting to feel like family.

Tears blurred Maya's vision. She stumbled, choking on the scream building in her chest. "Why does this always happen?" she cried.

Ethan's fists clenched, jaw trembling.

Robert grabbed them both. His voice, low but steady, stated, "We can't stay." "We grieve later. We survive now."

They ran—, but as they did, Robert said just loud enough for them to hear, "In a world this broken, we carry hope by not letting it die with them."

Maya and Ethan were quiet as they walked, the weight of their father's words settling deeper than the surrounding silence. Something shifted in that moment—not just grief, but a spark of resolve. They had cried; they had screamed, but now… now they understood. It wasn't just about surviving anymore. It was about honoring those who didn't make it. Keeping hope alive—for Maya, for Josh, and for everyone they'd lost.

A quiet strength rose in them, something new. A maturity shaped by fire.

By the next morning, the forest had thinned. The air felt warmer—softer even. The wilds gave way to open land, and in the distance, they saw the shimmer of something else. Roads. Rooftops. Civilization, or something like it. Spring had arrived in full, brushing green over the hills and trees as if trying to paint away the past.

Ahead lay the Emerald Zone.

It looked perfect from a distance. But they knew better than to trust appearances.

CHAPTER 7

THE EMERALD DISTRICT

The city's ruins fade in the rearview mirror as Robert, Maya, and Ethan press on toward the Emerald District. The road ahead is smoother, the landscape less ravaged, but tension lingers in the air.

Robert glances at his children, their eyes scanning the horizon. "Stay alert," he murmurs. "This place looks calm, but we can't let our guard down."

Maya nods, adjusting her jacket. "We blend in here, right? People live normal lives. We just need not to draw attention."

Ethan fidgets. "It's strange… tanks on the streets but no bombed buildings. Almost feels normal."

Robert cracks a smile. "That's the illusion. Remember, we're passing through. Keep your heads down."

As they approach the Emerald District, the orderly streets and functional homes stand in stark contrast to the chaos behind them. Soldiers patrol, but citizens move freely, exchanging wary glances. The family steps into this new reality, hearts pounding but faces calm. The Emerald District awaits, a silent promise of uneasy peace.

Their boots hit pavement—actual pavement—for the first time in weeks. Buildings stood tall and mostly intact, storefronts lined the streets, and artificial order hummed in the air. It was too clean. Too quiet. The Emerald Zone looked like a picture frozen in time, untouched by the war that tore through the rest of the country.

As they walked deeper into the city, the tension grew. Every sound made them flinch. Every glance over the shoulder felt like a threat. When a figure appeared ahead—an older woman in a gray shawl—they froze.

Ethan stepped in front of Maya instinctively. Robert reached slowly for his side, eyes narrowed.

But the woman just smiled. "You three look like you've been through hell," she said, her voice soft, worn, and kind. "Come on. Let's get you checked out."

They hesitated—but kindness like that was rare. Too rare to ignore.

At the local health post, someone checked their vitals. Radiation levels? Low. Thyroids? Stable. Blood pressure is slightly high from stress, but manageable. Undernourished, yes—but alive. And somehow, still whole.

The woman returned with clean clothes. Ethan got his haircut first, the shaggy ends falling away to reveal sharper features. Robert shaved in silence, the years seeming to melt from his face. Then Maya approached the mirror.

She looked at herself—dirt-smudged, sunburned, eyes tired but determined. "Do you have any brown hair dye?" she asked quietly.

The woman nodded and handed her the box.

It was time to blend in. Time to disappear.

For now.

Someone gave Maya, Robert, and Ethan a temporary residence near the center of the district after they cleaned up. It wasn't much—just a small flat with concrete walls, recycled furniture, and a screen near the door that pulsed with state-issued messages—but it was warm, safe, and quiet. Too quiet.

The neighbors spoke little. No one knocked. Smiles were tight, polite, and quickly withdrawn. Every few blocks, surveillance drones hovered silently, scanning faces, recording every move. Uniformed guards patrolled with calm, practiced menace.

"This place is like a stage," Robert muttered one evening, peering through the blinds. "Everything looks fine until you say the wrong line."

Maya sat at the table, running a hand through her now-dark hair. She barely recognized herself in the mirror. Ethan had already started studying the street patterns and guard rotations, keeping notes in the back of an old ration book. They weren't resting. They were preparing.

They knew—even here in the Emerald Zone—they were still being hunted.

They stood in silence, staring at the little house tucked between two polished walkways. It wasn't grand—just a modest, single-story home with clean windows, a garden out front, and soft light spilling from inside. But to them, it looked like something out of a forgotten dream.

After everything — the chaos, the blood, the winters, the mutants, the loss—this felt unreal.

Robert was the first to speak, voice cracked. "I haven't seen a home… not a real one… since the beginning."

Maya stepped closer, her hand trembling as she touched the doorframe. "It's been almost two years," she whispered. "Since we lost ours."

Ethan didn't say a word—he just stepped forward and pulled them both into a tight hug. All three of them held each other, shaking, breath catching in their throats.

"I wish Mom were here," Maya said, her voice breaking. "Even if this is just a fantasy."

Robert didn't move. "Is she still out there?" he asked quietly. "Has she found somewhere like this? Or is she gone? Changed? Could she even still be the same woman?"

They stood there in the doorway, a fragile moment of peace holding them together.

Maya clutched the necklace her mother used to wear that she found in the rubble of the last place she was before the war, fingers curling tight around the charm. Robert reached into his pocket and pulled out the old ring that his wife, Bridget, once wore. He stared at it, eyes damp, heart pounding. Remembering his love, remembering their wedding, marriage, engagement, and life before all of this.

Hope was a dangerous thing. But somehow, they still carried it.

Even now. The registration office was small, sterile, and too quiet. The place where everything echoed. The woman behind the desk barely looked up as she spoke. "Name and identification."

Robert stepped forward first. "Michael Turner," he said flatly.

The woman typed without looking. "Residence address?"

"Forty-seven Elm Terrace," he replied, praying it was still available in the system. They had given him one of the few safe names.

Maya's hands were stiff as she stepped up next. "Maya Turner," she said.

Ethan gave the name "Jacob" a voice a little too nervous.

The woman squinted for the first time, pausing just long enough to make Robert tense.

"These names aren't syncing yet," she muttered. "We're running system updates today. Come back tomorrow morning. Same time."

"Is there a problem?" Robert asked too casually.

"Shouldn't be," she said. "Just delays. We'll clear it."

As they turned and walked back toward the house, none of them spoke. Maya's heart pounded in her ears. She could feel sweat forming at her hairline. Robert kept glancing over his shoulder. Ethan walked a little too fast.

They were nearly on their block when a voice called out from the alley beside them.

"Hey."

All three of them turned, startled.

It was a man in his forties. Civilian clothes, but alert eyes. He stepped out of the shadows, holding a bag of groceries like any other neighbor.

"You're not from around here," he said, not unkind, but not friendly either. "People who aren't from here usually either disappear or… make someone else disappear."

Robert stiffened. "We're just passing through."

The man gave a slow, knowing smile. "Yeah, sure. Look… just a word of advice." He stepped closer, lowering his voice. "People talk. And right now, there's a rumor going around the zone about three fugitives tied to the resistance. Might want to watch your backs."

Then he turned and walked off as if nothing had happened.

The family stood frozen. Maya clutched her necklace. Ethan clenched his fists.

They hurried home, and the moment they shut the door, panic set in.

Robert locked every bolt. "We need to be ready," he said. "They might come tonight. Or tomorrow. But they're coming."

The next morning, they returned to the registration office—stiff, anxious, but trying to act normal.

The woman behind the desk smiled this time. A little too warmly.

"Good news," she said, her fingers tapping rapidly across her terminal. "We figured out the issue. The system flagged your names because of a recent cyberattack. Nothing to worry about—it happened to a lot of folks during the last purge. Some records got scrambled."

Robert exchanged a glance with Maya, who barely nodded.

The woman kept typing. "So we're going to assign you regional identities. Same name, new system profile, all synced to your address."

She turned the screen toward them with three digital ID cards forming on it—photos taken from the street cams, faces neatly cropped, information filled in.

"It'll take a day or two to fully update," she added. "But you're cleared to stay and move freely within Zone S-3 in the meantime."

Ethan blinked. "That's it?"

She smiled again. "That's it. War scrambled a lot of things. We're just trying to keep the city moving."

They left the building feeling light—but not safe.

Maya whispered under her breath as they stepped back into the sun. "It's too easy."

Robert's jaw clenched. "Exactly."

Ethan looked over his shoulder. "We just got loaded into a new system. With our actual faces."

They didn't run. Not yet.

But the clock had just started ticking.

Later that afternoon, they returned from the food depot, each carrying two large bags packed with supplies—bread, canned beans, rice, dried fruit, and powdered milk. No one stopped them. No payment, just an ID scan and a smile from the worker behind the counter.

Robert closed the apartment door and dropped his bags on the counter. "Too easy," he muttered.

Maya nodded as she unpacked. "We should prep. Fill our bags just in case."

Ethan loaded his pack with the heavier items. "And we've gotta stop being weird," he said, glancing toward the window. "We're being watched, even if it doesn't feel like it."

Robert sighed. "Alright. Let's play normal."

So they did. That evening, they stepped outside, walking casually down the street, past the humming streetlights and the trimmed hedges that looked too clean to be real. And right on cue, the man from yesterday stood at his fence, waving.

"Hello, neighbors!" he called, smiling.

They paused. Hesitant.

"I'm sorry about yesterday," he said. "We've had… issues in the past. So, we tend to test new arrivals. See if they're, y'know, stable. The Homeland Directory encourages it. Gotta keep the community safe."

Robert forced a polite nod. "We understand."

The man's smile widened. "My name's Randall. My wife makes a mean meatloaf. Apple pie, too. Are you three free tonight?"

Maya and Ethan exchanged glances. It was play along—or raise suspicion.

"Sure," Robert said slowly. "We'd be honored."

Dinner was warm. Comfortable, even. His wife, Teresa, was friendly and chatty. The meatloaf was perfect; the pie was rich with cinnamon. They all laughed at small jokes. Talked about the weather. Acted as if things were normal.

But when they returned home that night, the silence hit like a brick.

"Was that kindness?" Maya asked.

Ethan dropped onto the couch. "Or just a test?"

Robert didn't answer. He just looked out the window at Randall's house across the street—light still on, curtain swaying slightly.

"They're either trying to get close," he said, "or trying to lower our guard."

The next morning, sunlight filtered through the kitchen blinds, softer than it had been in weeks. For once, there was no shouting, no drones overhead, no reason to rush. Just quiet.

Robert stood at the counter, rubbing the sleep from his eyes while Maya rummaged through the cabinets. "This place is too clean," she muttered.

Ethan opened the fridge—nothing but sealed rations and a pitcher of filtered water. "Figures."

But then Maya froze, her hand resting on a half-open cupboard. "No way…" she whispered.

Robert turned. "What is it?"

She slowly pulled out a box, dust-covered but sealed. Pancake mix.

The exact brand their mom used.

Everything hit at once.

That morning in their old kitchen. The smell of pancakes on the stove. Their mom was humming that soft tune. Her smile as she said goodbye. The interview. The fishing job. The blast. The chaos. The world is tearing itself in half.

Maya's hands trembled as she set the box on the counter. Ethan stepped closer, eyes wide. "Is it…?"

"It's the same," she whispered. "It's the same."

Robert didn't speak. He just stared at the box, jaw tight, his fingers gripping the back of a chair.

Without a word, Maya pulled out a pan. Ethan grabbed plates. And for the first time in what felt like forever, they made pancakes.

They didn't cry. Not right away.

But when they sat down, steam rising from the stack in front of them, the silence was louder than any bomb.

"I wonder if she's eating right now," Ethan whispered. "Somewhere."

Maya looked down at her plate. "I hope it's pancakes."

A knock at the door.

All three froze. Robert slowly stood, motioning for Maya and Ethan to stay behind him. He opened the door just a crack—just enough to see Randall standing there, a little pale, eyes darting down the hallway.

"I have a warning," he said, voice low. "Two people were found dead in the zone this morning. Not far from the checkpoint. The rumor is… they weren't from here."

Robert's face didn't move. "What are you saying?"

Randall glanced over his shoulder, then stepped closer. "I need to ask—do you know anything about that?"

Behind him, Maya's stomach flipped. Ethan went still, his fingers tightening around the edge of the table.

Robert took a breath, then opened the door wider. "You ask a lot of questions, Randall. Come in."

Randall hesitated, then stepped inside. Robert gestured to the couch, then leaned on the table across from him.

"Yes," Robert said. "We knew them. But it's not what you think."

Randall's eyebrows raised, but he stayed quiet.

"They were two people we had met before we ever reached this zone. They weren't soldiers. They weren't killers. They were survivors, just like us. They tried to follow us, and they died for it. Ambushed. They didn't even have a chance."

"And you?" Randall asked carefully. "What are you running from?"

Robert's eyes didn't flinch. "We're running from what the world become. We're not here to stir up trouble. We just want to survive."

Randall leaned back slowly, watching him. "That story better be true."

"It is," Robert said. "And we've got nothing left to prove."

Randall stood. "I believe you… for now. But others might not. Be careful. The walls are thinner than they seem."

He left without another word.

The door closed. The tension stayed.

Maya looked at Robert. "Think he'll turn us in?"

Robert didn't answer immediately. "Not yet. But someone will."

The community-wide meeting was tense. People gathered in the square as officials spoke about maintaining peace, watching for resistance activity, and reporting anything unusual. It was dressed up as a "safety update," but the message was clear: the Emerald Zone wasn't as secure as it pretended to be.

When it was over, Maya leaned against a wall, arms crossed. "You know what we need?" she mumbled.

Robert raised an eyebrow. "More food? More gear?"

"No," she said. "A dog."

Ethan blinked. "A dog?"

"I'm serious," she said. "Something loyal. Something that warns us before people creep up. Something that's... ours."

So later that afternoon, they visited the pet district—one of the stranger luxuries of the Green Zone. Rows of kennels lined a white-walled shop, and behind the counter sat a tired-looking man with sharp eyes.

Robert pointed to a large, black-and-tan German Shepherd with a calm stare and battle-scarred ears. "That one," he said.

"She's trained," the man said. "Obedience, patrol, defense. Retired military dog. Still got a lot of fight in her."

They named her Raya.

That night, as she curled at the foot of their bed, Maya rested a hand on her warm fur.

"She's family now," she said. "Who's a good girl!" Maya encouraged Raya

And in a world full of danger, lies, and shadows—Raya would be the first to growl before the storm.

That morning, Randall walked calmly into the Homeland Security Department station.

"I have a report," he said. "Robert and his family. They're not who they say they are."

The officer barely blinked. "We know."

Randall hesitated. "You do?"

"We're letting them feel safe. When the time's right, we'll move."

That night, the air was still—too still. Then Raya, curled up by the front door, snapped her head up. Her ears twitched.

She growled.

Then barked—sharp and loud.

Robert rose from his chair, heart pounding. "Something's wrong."

Before anyone could move, gunfire ripped through the district.

A spotlight flared outside, followed by roaring engines and the screech of metal. Trucks—ramshackle, armored, and draped in dark cloth—burst through the Emerald Zone's western gate. Mounted machine guns opened fire, tearing through guards and civilians alike. Screams filled the air.

From atop the lead truck, a voice boomed through a speaker system, distorted and furious:

"Robert! We know you're here! Come out, traitor! You murdered our own!"

Maya pulled Ethan to the ground as a blast shattered their window. Raya barked again, then stood protectively over them.

Robert's face went pale. "They think I killed Maya and Josh…"

The cult surged through the streets, soldiers in black robes marked with blood-red serpents across their chests. The Serpent's Path—a splinter sect more violent and fanatical than the last.

Their leader stood tall on the truck, with wild eyes and a jagged crimson tattoo running down his face. Prophet Varek.

"We came for blood," Varek shouted. "We came for HIM!"

Belvarian occupation forces scrambled, outgunned and outmatched. Civilians, those who could, began fighting back, grabbing weapons from fallen guards or hidden stockpiles.

And amidst the chaos, Robert turned to Maya and Ethan.

"This is it. They know. Everyone knows."

Maya nodded. "So, what do we do?"

Robert looked out the shattered window.

"We run. We run now. And we don't stop until we reach the Yellow Zone."

Amid the screams and fire, as bullets ripped through buildings and families hid beneath shattered rooftops, Randall ran through the chaos, waving a tattered sheet of paper in his hand.

"I have a message! A message!" he yelled. "Prophet Varek—I know Robert! Please, stop this!"

The cult's trucks slowed. One gunman pulled Randall forward, forcing him before the prophet.

Randall held out the note, shaking. "He left this… I thought he was the enemy. But I was wrong."

Varek snatched the note from his hand, eyes narrowing as he read. It was in Robert's handwriting—rough, rushed, but sincere.

"To whoever finds this, I'm sorry. Maya and Josh weren't enemies. They were just survivors. We escaped the cult together, but Belvarian Occupation drones killed them when they tried to follow us. I intended to save them. I failed. I am not an enemy of yours. But I won't stop protecting my family." -Robert.

The Prophet's jaw clenched. His eyes scanned the burning city—his forces still firing, the people fleeing, the guards dying.

Slowly, he raised his hand.

"Cease fire!" he bellowed.

The guns fell silent. The fire still burned, but the roar of war stopped.

He turned to Randall. "This man… Robert. He's not who I thought. We came for vengeance… and we brought more death."

Without another word, the cult trucks pulled out—smoke curling behind them, silence chasing them into the night.

What remained of the Emerald Zone was no longer green. It was scarred. Burned. A broken promise.

An orange zone.

And yet, as civilians crawled from the rubble and pulled one another to safety… they remembered that what stopped the bloodshed wasn't guns or walls.

It was a man who chose truth, even when he was hated.

Robert didn't stay to see it. But his words had done what weapons couldn't.

As they walked away from the ruins, the sky beginning to shift from smoke-gray to morning gold, Maya glanced back.

"Do you think they survived?" she asked softly.

Ethan looked up at Robert, his voice barely above a whisper. "Do you think they made it?"

Robert paused, staring out over the hill. "I sure hope so."

Then, after a beat, he added, "Let's go check."

They crept through the treeline, back toward the edge of the town. The wind carried the smell of ash and damp earth—but no gunfire. No shouting. The smoke had thinned, and the fires were out.

From their vantage point, they saw movement—people clearing rubble, tending to wounds, reuniting. The walls had been patched, and guards now stood alert with steadier eyes.

And up on one of those walls stood Randall, holding a folded sheet of paper in his hand—the same note Robert had left behind.

He saw them on the ridge. He didn't shout. He didn't chase.

He just lifted the paper… and waved.

Robert stared for a moment, then gave the faintest smile.

"Well," he muttered, "I guess he's not so bad after all."

Maya looked up at him, smiling through the weight of everything.

Ethan adjusted his pack.

And together, they turned back toward the road.

The Emerald Zone was behind them.

But hope—just a sliver—still walked with them.

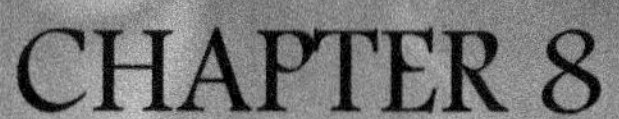

CHAPTER 8

THE BUMBLEBEE DISTRICT

They left the Emerald Zone behind them, but it didn't leave them. The smoke still clung to their clothes. The sound of gunfire echoed in their bones. And the silence… the silence after destruction was always the loudest.

The cracked, winding, and uncertain road lay ahead. They didn't know what the Bumblebee Zone held. But they knew it wouldn't be easy.

What mattered now was simple.

They were still together.

And they were still moving.

Summer had arrived, but it brought no peace. The sun hung heavy in the sky, casting a dry, golden glare over the crumbling skeleton of what once was a city. The roads cracked, and the sun bleached them. Heat waves danced above scorched rooftops and shattered glass.

This was the Yellow Zone—known to locals as the Bumblebee Zone. It buzzed with life, but not the kind that brought comfort. The buildings were half-standing, patched together with scrap metal, wood, and whatever else survivors could find. Old homes leaned like tired men. Shanties creaked with every gust of wind.

The air reeked of smoke, engine oil, and sweat.

Patrols marched through the narrow alleys in pairs—some masked, some not—clad in dull gray armor with batons at their hips and rifles slung over their shoulders. Eyes always watching. Propaganda blasted from mounted speakers on street corners, cycling messages about obedience, unity, and betrayal.

"Order brings survival. Loyalty brings peace."

It played every hour. No one listened anymore.

People moved with sluggish caution—heads low, voices quiet. Their tattered and sun-faded clothes showed. Kids played in the dirt with broken toys, too used to the sound of boots and drones to flinch.

The Yellow Zone wasn't lawless.

But it was forgotten.

And that, Maya thought, might be worse.

As they turned the corner, the sun beat down on the cracked pavement, blinding for a second—until they saw it.

Two civilians were on their knees near a burned-out bus stop, their hands raised, trembling. A soldier in dark gray armor circled them with a slow, deliberate swagger of power unchecked.

"Keep your hands up," he barked. "I'm checking to see ifyou'ree resistant."

"We—we promise we're not resistance," one of them stammered.

The soldier didn't even hesitate. "Did I tell you to speak?"

Then came the crack of the rifle stock—slamming into the man's shoulder, sending him sprawling. His wife screamed, but the soldier kicked them both to the ground without a second thought, his boots landing with sickening force.

Robert, Maya, and Ethan froze, ducking into a shadowed alley.

That's when it hit them.

This wasn't the Emerald Zone. This wasn't a place of false smiles and hidden threats.

This was the Yellow Zone—raw, exposed, and merciless.

And now, they had to survive it.

They pressed their backs against the cold brick wall of the alley; the shadows hiding their faces as the sound of boots faded down the street.

Maya's voice trembled, just above a whisper. "How are we going to survive this?"

She looked up at Robert, eyes wide, fear written all over her face. "They're going to find us. If they tracked us into the Emerald Zone, they'll definitely find us here. And they won't treat us fairly. Not here."

Robert didn't answer immediately.

Ethan leaned forward, his voice raw. "What are we going to do? Have we come to the end of our road, Dad?"

Robert turned, placed a steady hand on Ethan's shoulder, then looked at them both.

"No," he said firmly. "We aren't done. And we're not getting caught anytime soon."

He lowered his voice, eyes sharp.

"So here's what I need you to do—I need you not to be afraid. I need you to keep doing what you've already been doing. Stay strong. Stay sharp. Fear is your biggest enemy here. Not them."

He pointed down the alley, toward the broken buildings and narrow paths ahead.

"The moment you let fear take over is the moment you falter. Be brave. Whether or not I'm here, you carry the same boldness that's gotten you this far."

His tone hardened just slightly, just enough to stir a fire in their chests.

"And if they try us… We'll make them regret it."

Maya nodded slowly, her fists clenched.

Ethan looked up, eyes steadier than before.

And with that, they slipped deeper into the Bumblebee Zone—quiet as shadows, but ready for whatever came next.

A voice cut through the alley like a whip.

"Hey! What are you three doing? Get back to work!"

A Belvarian occupation soldier, helmeted and armed, stepped into view.

Robert didn't speak—he just grabbed Maya and Ethan's arms. "Move. Now."

They bolted down the alley, boots hitting broken concrete, ducking into a rusted-out store with half its windows shattered and its sign faded beyond recognition. The air inside was thick with dust and silence.

They ducked into corners, breath shallow.

The soldier followed. His boots crunched over broken glass as he stepped cautiously inside.

Robert's eyes never left him. He moved like a shadow—slow, deliberate, quiet.

The moment the soldier passed the broken shelving unit, Robert struck.

He grabbed him from behind, silencing him with one hand while driving his knife cleanly into the gap in the armor at the side of the neck. The soldier thrashed once, then went still.

Robert dragged the body into a back storage room, covering it under a collapsed tarp and shattered boxes.

He returned to Maya and Ethan, his face calm but cold.

"We need to move."

Maya stared for a second. "Is he—?"

"He won't be calling for help."

Ethan swallowed hard, then nodded.

They slipped back out into the alleys—shaken, but alive.

As they weaved through the alleys, ducking low behind broken fencing and hollow walls, a sharp screech erupted from the nearest street corner speaker.

A voice crackled to life—clear, firm, and cold.

"Attention, citizens of Zone S-2. Be on alert for three fugitives: Robert Warren, Maya Warren, and Ethan Warren. Images are being transmitted now. These individuals are enemies of peace and associates of terrorist resistance factions."

The screen above the speaker flickered to life, showing surveillance photos from the Emerald Zone—Robert clean-shaven, Maya with her dyed brown hair, Ethan newly trimmed.

"If seen, do not engage. Report immediately to your local Directory Outpost. They doubled the reward for capturing them or confirming their whereabouts to 500,000 credits.

Maya's breath caught in her throat.

"They know what we look like," she whispered. "Even with the changes."

Ethan glanced at the man across the street—tattered shirt, hollow eyes, clearly hungry. The man looked up at the screen, then slowly back down.

Robert's voice was calm, but heavy. "We're targets now. Not just for the soldiers. For everyone."

Down the street, more soldiers arrived. Trucks rolled into the district, unloading armored patrols and drones that buzzed high above the rooftops. The Bumblebee Zone had changed overnight.

No longer just poor.

Now it was dangerous.

And every hand might reach for the reward.

Inside the abandoned store, Maya crouched over the soldier's gear, her hands moving fast. She grabbed the pistol first, checking the magazine as Robert had taught her. Full.

Ethan found a vest under the fallen body. "It's a little beat up," he muttered, "but it'll stop something."

Robert nodded, taking the assault rifle and strapping it across his back. "We use what we can carry. Leave the rest."

Raya sniffed the gear, then padded back to the doorway, ears perked.

Maya found a helmet and slipped it on. It was too big, but it'd work for cover. She looked up at her father. "Are we really doing this?"

Robert looked back at her—then at Ethan—then toward the growing sound of boots in the distance.

"We don't have a choice anymore," he said. "This isn't about hiding now. It's about lasting."

They left the body behind and slipped deeper into the Bumblebee Zone, now armed and alert—no longer prey.

They slipped through another alley, their gear broken down and stuffed into worn-out bags, but their eyes sharp and pace tight. Every move was calculated. They had become ghosts—fast, quiet, and deadly.

Then the voice burst through the comms across the zone.

"There's a dead soldier in here! I repeat, we have a dead soldier— confirming identity now!"

"Roger. Terrorists have killed a soldier in the zone. Code red. Code red. Full lockdown. Sweep everything."

The air changed. The sound of boots pounding pavement grew louder. Drones whirred above. Sirens echoed between buildings.

Robert's eyes narrowed. "This is it."

No more hiding.

As they turned the corner and spotted a patrol unit moving in from the west, Robert shouted, "Contact!"

Maya was already up, taking the shot first—quick, clean. Ethan flanked left, firing from behind a rusted dumpster. Robert covered the rear, squeezing off bursts between breaths.

Alley to alley, they moved like a single unit—backpacks tight, guns drawn, shadows wrapped in heat and gunpowder.

They dropped another squad. Ethan rushed forward, pulling two grenades from a fallen soldier's vest. "Got 'em!"

"Bag 'em," Robert said, already checking ammo. "We'll need every piece."

Raya barked once, low and alert, before following close behind.

Every corner was a new battleground. Every shot they fired carved a line between survival and capture.

And now?

They weren't just fleeing anymore.

They were fighting back—with purpose, with fire, and with fury.

With their hearts pounding and sweat clinging to their skin, they pushed forward—corner after corner, street after street. The city was a maze of cracked stone, smoking debris, and chaos. Every turn was a question: Is this the end? Is this the one we don't make it out of?

They didn't stop.

They couldn't.

Gunfire echoed behind them. Ahead. To the sides. But they kept moving, firing when they had to, ducking when they could. The zone had erupted into open warfare, and they were at the center of it.

Then—around the next corner—there was a soldier. Too fast. Too close.

He raised his rifle—too late.

Raya launched forward, growling with fury, her jaws clamping down on the soldier's arm as he screamed and crashed to the ground. She didn't let up, biting and shaking until he went still.

"Good girl," Robert said breathlessly. "Let's move!"

They darted into a crumbling alley, kicking down the door of a long-abandoned apartment building. Inside, the air was thick with dust and quiet. They raced up two flights of stairs and crouched low in a darkened unit, guns still in hand, breath ragged.

Outside, the footsteps faded.

They'd lost the patrol.

For now.

Maya slid down against the wall, her hands shaking.

Ethan knelt beside Raya, stroking her head. "We made it," he whispered. "We actually made it."

Robert looked out the cracked window at the chaos below.

"This is just the beginning," he said.

They sat in the dim light of the apartment, the walls cracked, the air hot and heavy. Their backs were pressed against peeling wallpaper, weapons resting in their laps, sweat drying on their skin. The silence was a blessing—but it didn't last.

Maya wiped dirt from her cheek, her voice low. "This is worse than Jericho."

Ethan nodded, staring at the floor. "And we don't even have Paul and his wife to help us this time."

Robert leaned against the wall, eyes distant but sharp. "Yeah," he said. "But they taught us what to do."

He looked at them both, his tone steady. "Paul and his wife were resistance. Real ones. And honestly… by now, I don't think we could not be resistance, even if we wanted to."

He glanced at the window, then back at his kids.

"If they're going to label us as enemies, as rebels, then fine. But we're not doing this for a cause. We're not fighting for a flag or some idea."

He paused, then added, "We're in resistance because we have no other choice. Because we're surviving."

Ethan looked at his dad, a small, proud smile forming beneath the weight in his eyes. He sat up a little straighter.

"Then let's survive better than anyone else," he said.

Robert gave a nod. "That's the plan."

The apartment shook from distant blasts—loud, thunderous hits that rattled the broken windows and sent dust falling from the ceiling. Raya lifted her head and growled low.

"What now?" Maya whispered.

Robert crept to the window and peeked out. His eyes widened. "It's not the occupation…"

Ethan joined him, and together they watched as twenty resistance fighters stormed the street below, using cover fire and anti-tank weapons to light up the advancing APCs. A blast rocked the earth as one exploded in a ball of fire. Drones spiraled out of the sky, picked off with expert precision.

"It's the resistance," Robert said. "This is our chance."

They grabbed their weapons and bolted down the stairs, moving fast but carefully, hands raised high as they approached the fighters.

One of the resistance leaders—a woman with a scar down her jaw and goggles over her helmet—raised her rifle for a second, then lowered it. "You three? We were wondering what the hell was going on. We thought our cell had been compromised."

"No," Robert said. "That was us. We've been running since the Emerald Zone."

The woman nodded. "Well, hell. Come with us."

They led them down a half-collapsed side street and through a trapdoor beneath an abandoned laundromat. Inside was a hidden bunker—cramped but full of equipment.

"You can't stay," she said, not unkindly. "Our group has to remain small and mobile. But we can gear you up."

Within minutes, Ethan was handed upgraded ammo and tactical gear. Maya received a new vest, extra mags, and sidearm modifications for an AKM and M4.

Robert looked down at what they gave him: a rocket launcher and an M249 light machine gun. He looked up at the fighter. "You sure?"

She smirked. "You've made it this far. You'll need it where you're going."

Before they left, she pulled them aside one last time.

"The Red Zone… It's a wasteland. Radiation. Mutants. Patrols that shoot first and burn the rest. No one dares to go there. But you… I see it in your eyes."

She looked at each of them—Robert, Maya, Ethan. Even Raya, sitting steady at their feet.

"You'll survive. May God have mercy on your souls."

They stood once more at the edge of the world—a long, cracked road stretching into a wasteland of smoke, silence, and scorched earth. The Red Zone.

Before them lay twisted wreckage, scorched buildings, and a green-tinted haze of radiation thick in the air. It looked like the end of everything.

Then came the roar.

The wind screamed as a Belvarian Occupation gunship tore through the clouds above, rotors slicing the sky like blades. The moment it spotted them, its side-mounted guns opened fire.

"GO!" Robert shouted, pulling Maya and Ethan down behind a rusted, burnt-out truck as the road exploded around them.

Missiles streaked past, shattering the ground with thunder. A fireball erupted behind them, knocking debris in every direction. They sprinted, ducking between twisted vehicles, shattered signs, and collapsed road barriers.

A burst of gunfire ripped through a car just inches from Ethan's shoulder. Raya barked wildly, staying close to his side as they weaved through the wreckage.

"We're not gonna make it!" Maya yelled.

"We will!" Robert shouted back.

Another rocket screamed toward them—BOOM!—it missed by seconds, launching a sedan into the air and flipping it over their heads.

Their boots hit the ash-stained ground of the Red Zone as they pushed through the last cover point.

Behind them, the chopper swung low, preparing for another pass.

Robert knelt, pulled the rocket launcher from his back, and aimed.

"Get down!"

With a thundering WHOOSH, the launcher fired.

The missile streaked into the sky—and slammed into the gunship's side.

The chopper twisted, flames licking across its hull as it spiraled and crashed in the distance.

Silence returned—but it wasn't peace.

It was the breath before the next nightmare.

The Red Zone awaited.

They collapsed behind a shattered concrete barrier, the wind thick with ash and the burning stink of fuel still drifting from the wreckage in the distance.

Everyone was breathing heavily.

Raya paced in circles, growling low, unsettled by the smoke and noise.

Ethan sat with his back against the barrier, his hands trembling, eyes wide with panic.

Robert was crouched, staring down the road, chest heaving, weapon still raised—like he wasn't sure if it was over.

Maya sat in the middle of them all, quiet for a moment… then let out a dry, shaky laugh.

"Well," she said, "that's… two times. No—maybe three—I really thought we were done for."

No one responded right away.

They had been close.

Too close.

Ethan wiped sweat and dust from his face. "I couldn't even breathe when that rocket hit."

Robert finally lowered his weapon, glancing at both of them. "I know," he breathed. "But we made it."

The road ahead stretched into the radioactive mist. A land no one dared enter.

But they were here now.

Scared. Shaken. And still standing.

Maya looked up.

"One step at a time, right?"

Robert gave a faint nod.

"That's how we've made it this far."

CHAPTER 9

THE CRIMSON WASTES

They walked in silence, the chaos of the attack chopper now a fading memory behind them. But the deeper they stepped into the Red Zone, the heavier everything became.

The sky shifted gray, greenish, and low like a poisoned ceiling. The wind was dry and oddly still, carrying a metallic scent that clung to their throats.

Warning signs littered the crumbled entrance:

DANGER: HIGH RADIATION LEVELS.

NUCLEAR DETONATION SITE–AUTHORIZED PERSONNEL ONLY.

MUTATION ZONE–EXTREME BIOHAZARD.

DO NOT ENTER.

DO NOT ENTER.

Yellow tape flapped in the wind, torn and faded but still clinging to fences that no longer stood.

Ethan looked up at one sign, barely visible beneath rust and grime. "It's like this place wants to make sure you know it's the end."

Robert said nothing. Just kept walking.

Maya reached out and gently touched the edge of a shattered warning post. It was still warm from the sun, but cold in a different way.

Raya stayed close, ears pinned back, growling at shadows.

Ahead, the world changed. Buildings crumbled into skeletal ruins. Green slime and broken tech littered the cracked and melted streets. And something—somewhere—was growling in the distance.

They had entered the Red Zone.

No more hiding.

No more warning.

Just survival. Maya reached out toward a half-melted metal sign, its surface glowing faintly with a greenish sheen.

"Wait," Robert snapped. "Maya—don't touch that!"

She froze. He was already stepping forward, his voice urgent.

"Back. Now. All of you—back up!"

They moved fast, retreating several feet to the edge of the crumbled zone entrance.

Robert turned, eyes sharp, voice low but serious. "I forgot. We need to take radiation precautions—now."

Ethan looked confused. "I thought we had already passed the worst of it?"

Robert shook his head. "This is different. This is high-exposure territory. We've only been in it a few minutes, but that's enough to matter."

He dropped his pack and began digging through it. "Maya, Ethan— here." He pulled out iodine tablets and a small vacuum-sealed pack of dried seaweed.

"Take these. The iodine protects your thyroid. The seaweed binds to the same receptor. Just do it."

They took them without hesitation.

Robert looked around. "We also need masks. It doesn't have to be fancy, just something to keep the dust and airborne particles out. We can't breathe this stuff for long."

Maya looked out toward the crumbled skyline of the Red Zone. "We're already in it…"

"Only for a few minutes," Robert said, placing a mask over his face. "That gives us a fighting chance."

Ethan pulled his scarf up, voice muffled. "You think we'll be okay?"

Robert's eyes narrowed at the mist ahead.

"We'll be okay. But from here on out, every second counts."

As they stepped into the abandoned building, the air felt thick with a metallic tang, and the silence was almost deafening. Every step echoed, the sound of their boots squelching against the slimy green radioactive residue that dripped from the walls. The building looked like something out of a horror movie, dark and filled with the eerie groans of a structure long abandoned.

Maya gripped her AK-47 tightly, its flashlight beam cutting through the darkness ahead. Beside her, Ethan held his M4, eyes scanning every shadow, while Robert's M249 LMG rested firmly in his grip. The wind howled outside, but inside, the creaks and whispers of the building seemed louder. The oppressive sense of danger hung heavy in the air, mixing with the strange scent of radiation.

"We have to keep moving," Robert whispered, his voice steady despite the tension.

As they maneuvered through the building, shadows flickered past the edges of their flashlight beams, quick and unsettling. Low growls echoed from unseen corners, and Maya tightened her grip on her AK-47. Ethan's voice wavered as he whispered, "What is that? Are there monsters in here, Dad?"

Robert glanced around, steadying his kids with a calm, firm nod. "There could be," he admitted, "but that's what we have our guns for. We've come too far to turn back now."

They pressed forward, the eerie quiet broken only by their footsteps and the occasional distant scrape of something moving in the darkness. The building felt like an abandoned asylum, its once pristine walls now covered in green, radioactive slime. The overwhelming sense of dread clung to them like the musty air, but they moved on, driven by the hope that somewhere ahead lay a chance to reunite with Bridget.

Exiting the building, they stepped into a desolate landscape. A rusted sign loomed ahead: "The Crimson Wastes. Do Not Enter. Heavy Radioactive Zone Ahead."

As they looked out, toxic water teeming with green slime stretched across the wasteland. A stench of unknown toxicity filled the air, making them grateful for the CB-RN masks that shielded them from the worst of it. The howl of the wind almost seemed to have a voice, and the clouds overhead were thick and gloomy, casting a gross darkness over everything. It felt like another world, yet it was painfully clear this was still their own.

Downed trees, partially destroyed buildings, and twisted metal littered the landscape. It became clear this was a site of a nuclear attack, but they were only on the furthest edges of the blast radius. What lay ahead was sure to be far worse.

Robert's eyes scanned the desolate landscape, his voice calm but firm. "Oh, my Lord… This is a nuclear blast site."

Maya and Ethan shared a panicked glance. "Dad, this is what it looks like up close?" Maya's voice trembled, her grip tightening on her AK-47. Ethan nodded, swallowing hard. "We've seen the mushroom cloud… but not this."

Robert took a deep breath, his gaze steady. "I know this is terrifying. But we've made it this far. This wasteland… It's just one more obstacle. We have no other choice. We trust what we've learned, and the potassium iodide will protect us long enough. We'll get out before we absorb too much radiation."

Maya and Ethan exchanged determined looks. "We trust you, Dad," Ethan said, his voice still shaky but resolute. Maya nodded. "Let's do this."

After that, they shared a brief prayer. Robert's voice was low and steady. "You know, we've been going so long, we haven't really had time to pray. If ever there was a time, it's now." He closed his eyes, and Maya and Ethan followed suit.

"Lord God, protect my children and me. If it has to be, let my children out. Protect them and help us survive, just as You helped Your people throughout the Bible. Let Jesus be with us, and may the Holy Spirit guide us. In Jesus' name, amen."

"Amen," Maya and Ethan echoed, their voices soft but resolute. They rose, determination in their hearts, and stepped forward into the wastes.

Robert pushed the rusted boat into the toxic river, its hull creaking but surprisingly stable. Without a paddle, they improvised, using a long metal rod to push off the riverbed. The surrounding water bubbled ominously, but they kept their focus on reaching the other side.

As they drifted, Robert tried to lighten the mood. "You know, I never thought our survival skills would include punting across a radioactive river."

Maya chuckled, shaking her head. "Yeah, this isn't exactly how I pictured our family vacations."

Ethan grinned, looking at the murky water. "At least we won't have to worry about sunburn out here."

Robert laughed. "True. Just remember, no swimming. This water's a bit more intense than the hotel pool."

Ethan joked, " That's good. I used to play all those video games. Maybe I can use my skills now.

Maya, " yeah maybe your games were preparing for this. I'm sorry I ever gave you any trouble for playing all the time."

Ethan replied, " Don't sweat it, sis."

As they finally made it to the shore, Robert said, "Keep your guns up, eyes sharp, and heads on a swivel. This is not a game, as I'm sure you know."

"Yes, sir. We're ready," Ethan and Maya replied in unison, their voices carrying a hint of humor as they mimicked soldiers. Despite their young age, they were indeed seasoned by survival.

Instead of heading into the city of twisted metal and burned-out buildings, they decided to slip into the forest of the Crimson Wastes. The eerie silence was broken only by the rustling leaves and distant groans of the wind. Perhaps they'd find some sort of shelter, clues, or anything useful. The city could wait; they'd have to return eventually.

As they ventured into the forest, it was clear this wasn't an ordinary woodland. The towering redwoods, once majestic, now stood as bare, wooden skeletons. Their branches, stripped of leaves, reached into the sky like twisted fingers. The ground beneath their feet was a patchwork of burnt dirt, a light brownish hue, with charred remnants of what once was. Burned-out vehicles and cabins were scattered throughout, silent testaments to the destruction that had taken place.

In the distance, something caught their eye. A shape, barely visible through the haze, loomed ominously. It could spell trouble. They exchanged tense glances, knowing that whatever awaited them, they'd face it together. They pressed on, prepared for anything.

As they ventured down, the charred remains of the forest gradually gave way to towering redwoods, still marked by the blast but resilient. The air felt a bit clearer, and they spotted a settlement ahead. Maya, Ethan, and Robert exchanged wary looks. Another settlement could mean anything—friend or foe.

As they approached the makeshift camp, masked survivors armed with rifles stepped forward. "What are you guys doing out here?" one of them asked, his tone surprisingly friendly. "You're not from around here, I can tell. You don't know what you're getting into."

Relief washed over them as the survivors gestured them inside. "Come on through. I know we look scary, but we're not gonna hurt you."

Once inside, the leader turned to them. "I'm gonna teach you a thing or two about the Crimson Wastes."

The man looked at Robert's family with a welcoming smile. "I'm sorry; where are my manners? My name's Brian. What's yours?"

Robert, Maya, and Ethan introduced themselves, exchanging polite nods. "Nice to meet you," Robert said, still cautious but grateful.

Brian nodded. "We've been surviving here for a long time. We're one of the few groups who made it outside the blast radius—barely, as you can see. We've got a little food and water to share with travelers like yourselves. But you really don't know what you've wandered into."

He gestured around them. "There are mutants in these parts—bears, wolves, even deer, all glowing green, ready to infect you with radiation. And don't get me started on the Belvarian Belvarian Belvarian Belvarian Belvarian Occupation Forces' elite guard—they're out here trying to wipe out anyone who survived the attack."

Maya and Ethan's faces went pale, their eyes wide with apprehension. Even Robert, usually composed, couldn't hide the gulp as he remembered their past encounters with wildlife. Those experiences had been harrowing enough, but now it seemed the threats had evolved into something far more dangerous. A chill ran down their spines, a stark reminder of the peril that lay ahead.

Maya looked at Brian with a hint of hope. "Will we die from this radiation? I just have to know."

Brian shook his head. "Did you take potassium iodide and seaweed?"

"Yes, our dad always makes sure we do," Maya replied.

"Good. That'll help for now, but your body's still absorbing a lot," Brian explained. "We've got a special tea brew with potassium iodide and a few other ingredients." He took a sip himself, smiling reassuringly. "See? It's safe."

Robert nodded at his kids, and they each took a tentative sip. The warmth spread through them, easing their nerves. "This is how we've survived," Brian continued. "We might look a little dirty, but we're healthy."

Brian looked at Robert's family with admiration. "Wow, you're well-equipped. Not used to seeing kids with guns, but I can tell you all mean business. You'd take a mutant out in a second." He called his group over. "Look at these survivors!"

The group gathered, eyes wide in surprise. They hadn't seen anyone outside their circle in ages, let alone a family so prepared. Robert, Ethan, and Maya felt an unexpected warmth in the exchange. After so long in isolation, this simple human connection was overwhelming. They hugged, expressing gratitude.

"I know you won't stay long, but I can guide you through the Wastes. I know these parts like the back of my hand," Brian offered, glancing back at his group. They looked reluctant, but Brian was resolute. "If I don't make it back, keep things going," he said.

Brian hugged each of his group members tightly, their farewells heavy with emotion. "Thank you, Brian," one of them said. "We really want you to make it back, so don't talk like you're not going to. If anyone can, it's you."

With a final nod, Brian turned to Robert, Maya, Ethan, and their loyal dog, Raya. "Alright, let's get going," he said, leading them down a hill and into a hidden underground cave. "This is the wolves' den. They're out hunting now, but we usually place a charge of C4 here to keep them at bay."

He glanced at Robert and his family. "Make sure you're ready. We'll need all the firepower we've got." Raya, wearing her tactical vest and helmet, let out a low growl, ready for whatever awaited them.

Brian asked, So I assume you've been through a lot other than the Belvarian Occupation and seeing the mushroom clouds. Robert replied, "I think we've seen it all, from mushroom clouds to green, yellow zones, in and out of resistance camps." "We've also been in plenty of shootouts with marauders, Belvarian occupation forces, and dangerous wildlife." Ethan said, "We did see a mutant once, but he was harmless; he seemed to be dying in a drainage tunnel." Brian retorted," Haha, young one, yeah, some mutants do make it out of the crimson wastes, key word it was dying, y'all got lucky!" Maya responded, "Don't scare my brother, it wasn't too long ago we were watching cartoons in a middle-class home after breakfast our mom cooked for us." Brian answered, "I'm sorry, Ethan, but he needs to know I'm not the best when speaking to people,e a bit awkward if you will." Maya rejoined, "We are looking for our mom!" Ethan's face became saddened after hearing his mom mentioned.

Brian listened, his expression growing more determined. "You've been through a lot, haven't you? From the Belvarian occupation to resistance camps, and now this wasteland." He shook his head, impressed by their resilience.

"Well, you're not alone in that anymore," Brian said firmly. "We'll find her together."

The distant howls grew louder, then erupted into a cacophony. "Get ready!" Brian shouted. "They're coming!" The glowing-eyed wolves surged from the shadows, a wave of green-furred menace. Maya gripped her AK-47, Ethan his M4, and Robert his M249. Brian's sniper rifle was poised, and Raya, ever vigilant, bared her teeth.

Gunfire erupted, echoing through the forest. Bullets tore into the pack, but some wolves still closed in. One lunged at Raya, but she swiftly turned, taking down several attackers. Ethan narrowly dodged a snapping jaw, rolling to the side and firing in one smooth motion. The battle was fierce, but they fought as a unit, each member determined to survive.

The distant howls grew louder, then erupted into a cacophony. "Get ready!" Brian shouted. "They're coming!" The glowing-eyed wolves surged from the shadows, a wave of green-furred menace. Maya gripped her AK-47, Ethan his M4, and Robert his M249. Brian's sniper rifle was poised, and Raya, ever vigilant, bared her teeth.

Gunfire erupted, echoing through the forest. Bullets tore into the pack, but some wolves still closed in. One lunged at Raya, but she swiftly turned, taking down several attackers. Ethan narrowly dodged a snapping jaw, rolling to the side and firing in one smooth motion. The battle was fierce, but they fought as a unit, each member determined to survive.

As Brian rallied at his camp, his team scolded him. "Brian, we warned you not to go. What if you had been killed?"

Brian took the scolding in stride, nodding at his group. "I know, I know," he said, "but sometimes you gotta take risks." The seven members joined Robert and his family, forming a larger, united front. As they made their way toward the town, everyone was on high alert, ready for whatever awaited them in the shadows.

Robert and the group approached a seemingly abandoned town. "Whoo, Robert signed, feeling a sense of relief as nobody was in the town. Robert's relief was short-lived as Brian's group exchanged wary glances. "This place might look empty," Brian said, "but trust me, there's always something lurking." The group pressed forward, eyes sharp, hearts pounding, knowing the Crimson Wastes rarely offered safe passage.

The town lay before them, a ghostly relic frozen in time. Storefronts stood silent, their windows cracked and coated in dust, with green goo dripping ominously from awnings and ledges. The streets, cracked and overgrown, whispered tales of a forgotten era. Everything felt eerily still, the only movement being the occasional flicker in the shadows. This small, abandoned town near the Crimson Wastes was a haunting reminder of a world left behind.

Brian glanced around, keeping his voice low. "We've never ventured this far before, not with the wolf packs. But it's as good a place as any to look for supplies." He signaled for the others to spread out, their steps careful and deliberate as they began to search through the deserted buildings.

The sharp sound of breaking glass echoed through the silent streets, freezing everyone in place. The once still air now felt charged with tension, as if the town itself was holding its breath. Shadows seemed to deepen, and the group exchanged wary glances, knowing that something unseen might be drawn to the disturbance.

Brian crouches low, his sniper rifle nestled into his shoulder. The wind howls, rattling broken glass in the abandoned buildings. He adjusts his scope, then lowers it to his binoculars. His breath catches.

Brian (into comms):

"...Hold up."

Through his binoculars, he sees it. A humanoid form steps out from behind a crumbling school bus—tall, thin, its skin pale and rotted, veins glowing sickly green. Patches of hair cling to its scalp, and its lifeless green eyes flicker.

Brian (low, tense):

"...First one's here."

He exhales, aims, and fires. The shot cracks like thunder, echoing across the ghost town. The mutant's head snaps back, collapsing.

Brian (into comms, urgent now):

"Mutants inbound. Horde status. MOVE. We've gotta MOVE NOW!"

Robert spins around, hearing the call. Maya and Ethan turn as growls fill the air. Mutants—dozens—begin flooding the streets. Some crawl from sewers, others leap off rooftops, all of them snarling, eyes blazing green.

MAYA (raising her AK):

"They're everywhere!"

ETHAN:

"I count twenty—no, thirty!"

Robert (calm but sharp):

"Circle up! Shoot to kill!"

Gunfire erupts. Muzzle flashes light up the dim street. Brian picks off mutants from above with rapid precision. Maya lays into a wave of them with short bursts. Ethan moves like a soldier, disciplined and fast.

Reznor fires his shotgun, backing into cover with the others. Raya, the loyal dog, rips into a mutant that gets too close.

Brian (over comms):

"We can't hold! We've gotta fall back!"

The group retreats through a narrow alley, emerging at the edge of the wastes. Just as they think they've cleared it—

The ground trembles.

A low rumble. Then a roar like a thunderclap. The sky seems to shiver.

From the top of a hill, a massive ten-foot bear steps into view. Its fur is mangled and dripping with green slime. Its eyes glow like molten emeralds. It stands on its hind legs, towering.

MAYA (horrified):

"…What is that?"

Brian (in disbelief):

"No. No, no… that's a prime. We call those things primals."

The bear roars again, loud enough to crack windows. The horde pauses—some mutants hiss and lurch toward it. The bear charges them instead.

It swings a massive claw, slashing five mutants in half in one swipe. Its teeth crush another. Blood and green slime fly.

ROBERT:

"It's giving us a shot—RUN!"

The group bolts through the open side of the field, mutants falling behind. But the bear turns… and sees them.

Its massive head lowers. It begins to chase.

Ethan (panting):

"It's coming after us—what do we do?!"

MAYA (breathing hard):

"Keep running! Dad!"

ROBERT:

"Go! Don't stop—just MOVE!"

Behind them, the roar grows louder, closer, and more furious. The ground shakes as the primal bear tears through buildings, locked on its new prey.

Everyone dropped to one knee, weapons raised, hearts pounding as the primal bear thundered toward them. Brian's voice rang out in the chaos, commanding the team to fire. Gunfire exploded all around. Muzzle flashes lit up the dark, painting the bear in bursts of light as bullets slammed into its massive frame. Still, it kept charging—unfazed, unflinching.

Brian's crew unleashed everything they had. Rifles barked, shotguns roared, and someone emptied an entire clip from a light machine gun. Maya's AK-47 rattled as she fired in controlled bursts, Ethan's M4 snapped with deadly precision, and Robert's M249 unleashed a steady stream of rounds. They aimed for the chest, the head, the legs—anything to slow it down. Nothing worked.

Brian took a deep breath and lined up the perfect shot with his sniper. He squeezed the trigger. The bullet hit the bear right between the eyes.

It barely blinked.

Instead, it growled louder, the sound rolling like thunder across the open land. Slime oozed from its eyes and jaws as it lowered its head and picked up speed, tearing through the terrain like a freight train of death.

The team stared in disbelief. Brian's voice cracked as he shouted for them to move. There was no time to think, no more chances to fight. They turned and ran, weapons swinging at their sides, boots pounding the cracked earth. The bear smashed through vehicles and crumbling stone as if they were nothing.

"There's nowhere to hide," Maya shouted between gasps, panic rising in her throat.

"Then we make a stand," Ethan snapped back, barely able to keep pace. "Or we don't make it."

The bear roared again, shaking the very air. And with that, the chase continued—relentless, hopeless, and closing in.

Robert, Maya, and Ethan scrambled up to a higher level on the ridge, slipping over loose rocks and broken concrete as the primal bear closed the distance. Brian vaulted up beside them, panting hard, rifle slung over his shoulder. Below, his team had gotten caught in the open valley—no time, no cover, no chance to escape. But they didn't run.

They stood their ground.

Gritting their teeth, they opened fire with everything they had—assault rifles, SMGs, even sidearms—letting loose with a fury that echoed through the wastes. The roar of their gunfire clashed with the monstrous growls of the charging beast, but still, they held.

One of the women grinned through the fear. "If this is how we go out," she said, her voice steady, "then I'm glad we didn't die starving in a hole."

Another man nodded beside her, reloading as fast as he could. "Mutated bear, nuclear wasteland… at least it's not boring."

They laughed—not because they weren't scared, but because they refused to let fear own their final moments. These were survivors of the blast. They'd seen cities fall, seen their world burn. And now, if death was coming, they'd face it together.

Clip after clip was emptied, the last stand of Brian's team written in fire and grit.

And above them, on the ridge, Robert could only watch with clenched fists as his friends gave everything they had. The bear charged forward, undeterred, tearing through gunfire like smoke.

Then it reached them.

And the ridge went quiet.

The bear slashed with wild, monstrous fury, its claws tearing through armor, flesh, and bone as Brian's team held their ground to the bitter end. Screams mixed with the roar of gunfire. One by one, the brave survivors fell—men and women who had already endured a nuclear apocalypse, now being torn apart by something not of this world. Brian, watching from the ridge, felt his heart collapse inside his chest. Guilt surged through him. He had brought them here. He had asked them to help.

His hands trembled as he pulled the trigger, shot after shot, driven not by duty anymore, but by grief and rage. Maya, Robert, and Ethan fired beside him, but their faces were pale, their eyes wide—not just with fear, but recognition. They'd seen this before. New friends, brave people, hopeful allies—gone. Not again. Not like this.

Robert's ankle gave out as they backed up the slope, forcing him into a limp. Maya and Ethan moved on either side of him, supporting him, their weapons still hot. They didn't speak, but the look they exchanged said it all: we can't save everyone.

"We have to push the boulders," Brian said through clenched teeth. "It's the only way."

Together, they pressed up the steep ridge. One by one, they rolled the massive rocks over the edge. The boulders tumbled down the slope and slammed into the bear below, slowing it—jolting it. It roared again, stumbling as green slime spilled from its wounds. But it kept coming.

Brian stopped. He didn't move another step.

"Go," he said, quiet at first. "GO!"

He turned, yanked the machete from his sheath, and charged. Robert tried to shout after him, but Brian was already halfway down the ridge. He slammed into the bear's side, swinging with everything he had. The blade cut into the creature's hide once, twice, three times. Blood and slime flew, but the bear roared, enraged, and swatted Brian across the rocks.

He fell, groaned, then staggered to his feet and struck again—right in the bear's eye. The bear reeled, grabbed him in one massive clawed hand… and hurled him from the mountain.

Robert turned away, eyes full. Maya held her breath. Ethan went quiet.

But the bear staggered now—limping, wounded, furious but slowed.

Brian's death wasn't in vain.

The family reached a small clearing near the ridge. There, carved into the rock, was a narrow cave entrance. They slipped inside, Robert nearly collapsing as he leaned into the wall, clutching his twisted ankle. The cave was dark and cold, but it was shelter. It was safe—for now.

They didn't speak. They just sat there, breathing heavily, weapons clutched in shaking hands.

They knew deep down that nothing would be the same after this.

This was the moment everything changed.

Brian, caught in the crushing grip of the primal bear, screamed as he slashed one final time—driving his blade deep into the creature's glowing eye. The bear let out a thunderous roar and hurled him off the ridge. His body disappeared into the abyss, leaving only silence behind. But his final blow had done real damage. The bear bled heavily now, stumbling as it turned its fury back toward the others.

Robert limped, his ankle throbbing with every step, but he didn't stop. Maya and Ethan flanked him, all three unloading their weapons as they climbed higher onto the mountain's edge. Bullets slammed into the bear's shoulders and chest, but it kept coming, slowed but enraged.

At the top, they found it—a small clearing surrounded by jagged stone, and behind it, the mouth of a dark cave. No escape. This would be it. Their final stand.

The bear charged, letting out a roar that shook the mountain. It slammed into them like a wrecking ball, throwing Maya and Ethan aside like rag dolls. Robert raised his machete, swinging wildly, slashing at its legs and side, doing whatever he could to hold it back. It swiped at him, knocking the blade from his hand.

Maya rolled across the dirt, spotted the machete, and without hesitation, snatched it up. With a shout, she leapt onto the bear's back and drove the blade down into its spine. The beast howled and reared up, flinging her into the air. She crashed to the ground, groaning but alive.

Ethan fired round after round, blood streaming down his face. The bear charged again, and this time, Robert dove for the machete. The monster lunged forward, jaws wide, ready to finish it.

But Robert struck first.

With one final cry, he drove the machete upward, plunging it deep beneath the bear's jaw, into the thick, pulsing flesh of its throat. The bear let out a final gurgling roar, then collapsed forward—dead.

The mountain went still.

Robert lay there panting, covered in blood and slime. Maya crawled over, clutching her ribs. Ethan knelt beside them, breathing hard.

It was over.

The monster was dead. But what it took to survive—what they lost—would stay with them forever.

Robert crawled from beneath the massive, steaming corpse of the bear, every muscle in his body aching, his breath ragged. He pulled himself to his feet, helped Maya up, and then Ethan. Without speaking, they turned toward the dark mouth of the cave and pressed forward— limping, bruised, bloodied. Relief washed over them, but it was a cautious kind, like they knew better than to trust it.

They had made it through the Crimson Zone—or at least another brutal piece of it. Somehow, again, they came out on top. But survival didn't feel like victory anymore. It felt like a curse.

Maya suddenly stopped, fists clenched, shoulders trembling. "Why does this keep happening?" she shouted, her voice echoing off the damp cave walls. "Oh, my goodness. Are you serious? Another bear? Wolves? Mutants? What's next?" She kicked a loose rock, sending it skittering. "I am so sick of this trash, trash, trash apocalypse!"

Ethan threw his rifle against the cave wall. The metal clanged sharply. "Me too!" he shouted, voice cracking from exhaustion and rage. "I hate this place! I hate it!"

They were breaking. Both of them.

Robert stood still for a moment, jaw clenched, eyes burning. Then he let out a growl and slammed his fists against the cave wall. Once. Twice. Again. Blood began to smear across the stone. He didn't care.

The three of them stood in the shadows, panting, furious, hurting— but alive.

Barely.

And as the echoes of their frustration faded into silence, so did the last bit of innocence they'd carried with them.

Suddenly, a low hiss echoed from deeper within the cave. It wasn't wind—it was breath. Wet, broken, ragged breath. Then came the scraping… the unmistakable sound of claws against stone.

Maya froze, her anger replaced by dread. Ethan stiffened, reaching for his rifle, but it was still lying against the wall where he'd thrown it. Robert turned, blood dripping from his fists, and slowly pulled his sidearm.

From the shadows ahead, figures emerged—twisted, twitching silhouettes crawling along the walls and ceiling like insects. Their eyes glowed faintly green, their limbs disjointed and malformed, as if melted and reshaped by the radiation. Veins pulsed visibly under their translucent skin. One of them opened its mouth and let out a deep, wet gurgling growl.

"Not again," Maya whispered, her voice hollow.

They came fast—no slow creep this time. These mutants had adapted to the dark. They thrived in it.

Robert fired first, his pistol cracking like a flare in the gloom. Ethan scrambled to recover his weapon, heart pounding, while Maya raised her machete, blood still coating the blade from the bear.

There was no time to mourn. No time to breathe.

The Crimson Zone wasn't finished with them yet.

They trudged on into the next stretch of the Crimson Wastes, wet clothes clinging to their bodies, the cave still echoing behind them. With their boots squished with every step, the soaked fabric did little to shield them from the chill wind that swept across the open terrain. But they didn't care. The slime was gone, the grit and blood washed away, and the brief comfort of the oasis gave them just enough strength to move forward.

The pool had saved them. One to cleanse, the other to drink—an impossible gift in a world like this. They hadn't stripped down, too paranoid to be that vulnerable, but the water had still done its work. The radiation clinging to their clothes and skin had started to fade.

Without the tea, the masks, and the seaweed, they would've already collapsed. Their anger, their trembling, the near-breakdowns—it wasn't just trauma. It was the weight of the radiation in their blood, their bones. But they were still alive.

And now they had a purpose.

"If we've been through all this," Maya said, her voice steady despite the exhaustion, "we have to find Mom. We have to."

"I agree," Robert said, his hand tightening around the grip of his machete. "We didn't come this far just to fall short."

Ethan looked at them both, his expression hard. "I'm with you. Whatever it takes."

The sun was beginning to set again, casting long red shadows across the wasteland. They didn't know what was ahead, but they had each other. And they had one goal left in this shattered world.

They would find her.

No matter what.

Maya, Robert, and Ethan stepped onto the charred edge of the nuclear city—the epicenter of the blast. Twisted metal rose in jagged, unnatural shapes all around them, skyscrapers leaning like skeletons, streets fractured with glowing green veins of radioactive slime. They had avoided this place for so long. Brian had warned them not to come here. They had listened. They had chosen the woods.

And now, after everything they'd endured, they wished they had come here first.

The woods had broken them. The bear, the mutants, the radiation, Brian's death. All of it weighed heavily on their backs as they stepped deeper into the skeletal ruins. But they weren't the same family that had entered the Crimson Wastes. Something had changed.

A mechanical buzz cut through the silence. They looked up.

Drones.

Three of them zipped through the sky—sleek, angular, with red glowing eyes and weapon mounts spinning beneath them.

Maya's jaw tightened. "Oh no. Belvarian Belvarian Belvarian Belvarian Belvarian Occupation Special Forces."

Robert scanned the sky. "Brian said their elite guard was stationed near here…"

Ethan raised his rifle, the old hesitation gone from his eyes. "Then we make them pay."

They had thought they were part of the resistance. They were told they were fighting for freedom. But now, they saw the truth. The Belvarian occupation had caused this—the radiation, the broken cities, the loss of their mother. It was their war, their bombs, their monsters.

Now it was personal.

As the drones flew past, the family slipped into the shadows. Patrols marched along the streets below, dressed in black tactical armor, scanning the area with laser sights and barking orders in distorted voices.

Robert, still limping slightly, led the way to a rusted truck. Maya placed the C4 along its undercarriage while Ethan kept watch. When the patrol approached, they detonated it—an eruption of fire, smoke, and twisted metal that knocked several of the elite guard to the ground.

The city lit up with gunfire.

The elite forces responded quickly, their weapons far more advanced—plasma bursts ripping through the air, sparking against ruined cars and concrete. The trio ducked into a skyscraper, kicking down the broken doors and charging inside.

The interior was worse than the outside—dingy, full of dust and rot, the walls streaked with dried slime that pulsed faintly green. They moved up the stairs quickly, gunfire echoing behind them, boots pounding up the building after them.

On the top floor, they paused—breathing hard, soaked, shaken, but alert. Ahead of them stood an old industrial elevator. Its panel flickered weakly, humming with unstable power. Somehow, it still worked.

"Elite guard must've retrofitted it," Robert said, staring at it warily.

Maya wiped the sweat from her face, eyes locked on the panel. "Let's see if we can go up one more time…"

And they stepped forward, ready to ride the machine deeper into the heart of the enemy's stronghold.

As the elevator opened with a groaning hiss, the dim light inside flickered, casting long shadows on the cracked walls. Maya stepped in first, her rifle lowered but still tight in her hands. She took a deep breath, trying to calm the pounding in her chest. "We have to survive," she said softly, more to herself than anyone else. "No matter what."

Robert followed behind her, his voice low but steady. "We can never let ourselves get that angry again. We can't let this world twist us like it's twisted them. We keep surviving, yeah—but we do it with hope. We hold on to something good, something real. The hope in God has to stay with us. That's the only way we stay human."

Ethan stood at the doorway for a moment, watching the two people he loved most. The pain on their faces. The strength in their voices. He didn't say anything, but he felt it settle in his chest—like a fire being carefully relit. He nodded silently and stepped into the elevator.

As the doors slowly closed behind them, sealing them in the flickering light, none of them knew what would be waiting at the top. But they had already made it through death and fury. Now, they had a purpose. And no matter what came next, they were going to face it together.

As Maya opened the first door at the end of the corridor, she barely had time to react. A crushing force hit her square in the chest, sending her flying back. Ethan was slammed to the floor beside her, and the sound of boots filled the hall as masked elite soldiers stormed in. Black armor, red visors, no hesitation. Rifles raised, commands barked.

Their weapons were yanked from their hands. Ethan struggled, only to be thrown against the wall, his face twisted in pain. Maya kicked and fought, but one of the soldiers struck her in the ribs, knocking the wind from her lungs. Robert rushed to help—but a blow to the head sent him crashing to the floor, blood already trailing down his temple. His weapon was stripped away before he could even lift it.

They were dragged across the room like prisoners, shoes scraping against metal and stone. A wide industrial chamber opened up before them, dark and cold. And in the center of it—flanked by a line of perfectly still soldiers—stood a tall man in a crisp black overcoat with the emblem of the League seared into his chest plate.

General Kael Varnak.

The Purifier.

He stepped forward, not rushing, not raising his voice. His face was emotionless, clean-shaven, with eyes sharp and hollow. A walking execution. A man who believed in what he did.

"I've been watching you, Robert," he said, almost calmly. "You thought you got away. Even in the resistance camps… of course, we have spies there. We have spies everywhere."

Robert's head throbbed as he was pulled up to his knees.

"We knew when you entered the Green Zone. We watched you in the Bumblebee District as well. And I'm sure you'll be pleased to know that every soldier who failed to eliminate you has been executed. As well as anyone you've come in contact with. Collateral… for your defiance."

Maya's chest rose and fell as she stared down at him, righteous anger burning in her eyes. Ethan lay beside her, wounded but alert.

Varnak stepped closer, boots echoing across the steel floor. "And your dear Bridget… I haven't found her yet." He paused. "But I will."

He leveled his sidearm at Robert's face.

"Your time is over. Your survival is a stain on this world."

Robert lifted his chin, glaring through the blood on his face. "If you're going to shoot me, shoot me."

Varnak tilted his head slightly, smiling faintly. "No," he said. "That's too easy."

He turned suddenly, aimed at Ethan—and pulled the trigger.

The gunshot cracked through the room. Ethan gasped as the bullet tore through his side, collapsing with a strangled cry.

"NO!" Maya screamed, throwing herself toward him. "ETHAN!"

Robert shouted in agony. "NO!"

But Varnak stood, calm as ever. "Yes," he whispered. "That's exactly what I like to see."

"You will die!" Maya spat, shaking with rage. "You have made the biggest mistake of your life!"

Robert, through clenched teeth, managed, "Maya… calm down. Don't give him what he wants."

Varnak gestured without a word. Two soldiers stepped forward and slammed their fists into Robert's gut, dropping him. They kicked him as he fell, beat him until he could barely move, then dragged his limp body across the floor like trash.

Maya reached for her brother, holding his hand as soldiers restrained her. Tears mixed with fury on her face.

Varnak gave one last look as Robert was dragged toward the exit. "You will see the end soon enough," he said coldly.

They hauled Robert up to the rooftop, cuffed him tightly, and forced him into the back of a military helicopter. As its blades spun to life, the wind whipped across the rooftop, drowning out the sound of Maya's voice as she screamed after him.

And then, he was gone.

Maya dropped to her knees, her hands shaking as the helicopter blades disappeared into the sky. Her eyes stayed locked on the space where her father had just been. Her voice broke apart as she screamed, "No, no, no, no, no! It can't be! We lost Mom, and we don't even know if she's out there… and now you're—" Her voice cracked as she looked down at Ethan, her baby brother.

He looked up at her, tears spilling down his face, lips trembling. "I love you," he whispered.

Maya's heart shattered.

"Please find Dad… and Mom… if you can," he said, his voice barely audible. "This might be the end for me. I love you, big sister."

And then his eyes closed.

"No!" she gasped, grabbing him. "No! Ethan!" Her voice echoed through the ruined halls, swallowed by the silence left in the helicopter's wake. She clutched him, trembling, unable to breathe. For a moment, it all caved in—everything they had survived, everything they had lost. Her body shook with sobs.

But she didn't let go.

She knew her father. He prepared for everything. And thank God— the bag was still there.

Wiping her tears with trembling hands, Maya pulled it close and tore it open. Her training kicked in, her hands moving through the supplies quickly. She lifted Ethan's shirt—blood-soaked through, but the bullet had passed clean through. No shrapnel. No fragments. It was a chance.

She grabbed a chest seal, tore it open with her teeth, and slapped it over the entry wound, pressing it down firmly. Her fingers moved to the exit wound, applying another seal and bandaging it tight. Her hands moved on instinct now—just like Robert taught her.

Then she reached into the side pocket, pulled out the cauterizing tool—a compact, battery-powered rod designed for battlefield trauma. She activated it; the tip glowed white-hot. Without hesitation, she pressed it against the edge of the wound. Ethan didn't scream—he was already unconscious—but the smell of burned flesh filled the air.

Maya winced, tears still falling, but she didn't stop.

"I've got you," she whispered. "You're gonna make it. You have to."

The fire of determination burned in her chest now, stronger than fear, stronger than grief. Her dad was taken away. Her brother was barely hanging on. Her mother's fate was still a mystery.

But Maya wasn't a child anymore.

She was going to get them all back. One step at a time.

Maya sat beside Ethan, her knees scraped and her arms trembling, but she kept her focus. She opened the bag again, digging through the supplies until she found one of the ration bars Robert had packed. It was dense, dry, but loaded with calories—just what Ethan would need once he came around.

She broke a piece off, softened it with a bit of water from the second bottle they had saved, and gently pressed it to his lips. He didn't respond. His body was still, unmoving, but his chest rose and fell in a steady rhythm. His heart was beating. That alone gave her hope.

She tilted his head gently and poured a little water into his mouth, letting it drip slowly so he wouldn't choke. It trickled down, and for a moment, she saw his throat swallow reflexively. Not much—but enough.

Relief washed over her like a wave. She sat back, closed her eyes, and let out a slow, shaky breath.

"He's still with me," she whispered. "He's still here."

Wiping her face with the sleeve of her shirt, Maya took one last look around the dim hallway, then pulled Ethan close, shielding him from the cold air and the dust. She knew they couldn't stay there long—but for now, for this moment, it was enough.

He was alive. And that meant the fight wasn't over.

The helicopter descended onto the edge of a sprawling work camp—rows of tents, rusted shacks, barbed wire fences, and thousands of prisoners hunched over machines, hauling debris, and digging trenches. The sky above was choked with smoke and the scent of oil, sweat, and suffering. Guards patrolled in black armor, rifles in hand, watching everything with cold, indifferent eyes.

As soon as the skids touched the ground, the door flung open. General Varnak stood tall, unmoved by the storm of dust the rotors kicked up. He grabbed Robert by the collar and yanked him forward.

Without ceremony, he shoved him from the chopper. Robert hit the ground hard, rolling in the gravel and dirt. Varnak stepped out behind him, knelt briefly, and unlocked the cuffs. They snapped open and fell at Robert's feet.

The general stood over him, then kicked him in the ribs just hard enough to leave a message.

"Get to work," he said flatly, his voice stripped of all emotion.

Robert coughed, then pushed himself to his knees. He looked up at the towering walls, the endless line of prisoners, the hopelessness etched into every face.

But he wasn't hopeless.

Slowly, he stood, facing Varnak directly, battered and bruised but with fire still in his eyes. "Just like my daughter said," he growled, his voice raw. "You're a dead man walking. You just wait. Your kind won't last much longer."

He took a step closer, never breaking eye contact.

"I know it's not right... But I'll be glad when you're gone."

Varnak stared at him, unflinching, as the gate behind Robert slammed shut and locked with a loud metallic clang.

Robert didn't turn back. He walked into the camp with purpose, fists clenched, heart steady.

The fire hadn't gone out.

It was just getting started.

CHAPTER 10

WE MEET AGAIN

Maya and Ethan sat quietly beneath the overhang of a broken wall, the air still heavy with dust and the weight of everything they'd been through. From the canteen tucked deep in the side pocket of Maya's pack, they each took a slow sip of Brian's tea—bitter, earthy, but familiar. This is the last of it. Just enough to ease the radiation that still clung to their bodies like ash.

They moved quietly, avoiding patrols, sticking to the shadows as they slipped out of the Crimson Wastes. The land began to shift—less slime, fewer twisted beasts, and more signs of decayed civilization. The edge of the Bumblebee Zone.

Not far from the checkpoint roads and long-abandoned farmlands, they found it: a small building with boarded-up windows and a rusted roof. It sat crookedly beneath the canopy of trees, quiet and forgotten, but solid enough to offer shelter. Maya swept through it quickly, checked the back exits, and cleared the rooms.

It would do.

She set Ethan up with what little food they had left, laid out blankets near a corner that stayed dry, and made sure his wound was sealed and clean. He watched her, his face pale but steady.

"You're gonna have to stay here," she said gently, brushing his hair back from his face. "Just for a little while. I've got to go find Dad."

Ethan looked up at her, his voice small but sure. "You'll come back?"

Maya smiled, holding his gaze. "I promise. But you have to stay quiet. Don't open the doors. Don't let anyone see you. I love you."

"I love you too," he said, voice trembling just a little.

She gave him one last hug—tight, protective—then rose, slung her rifle over her shoulder, and stepped into the fading light.

She didn't look back. She couldn't.

She had a promise to keep.

Maya's boots dragged through the dirt, legs heavy, clothes torn and dusted with ash. Two weeks of searching. Two weeks of walking back roads, creeping through abandoned fields, sleeping in ditches, and hiding from drones. She was exhausted, starved, and running on pure instinct—but she kept going.

And then… she found it.

Hidden behind the forest line outside the Bumblebee Zone, surrounded by layers of fences and towers, stood the prison. Massive. Silent. Dreadful. Maya crouched behind a tangle of trees, her breath catching in her throat as she peered through the brush. She saw it. A figure among the workers—limping, sunburned, but unmistakably him.

Robert.

Her father.

She pressed a hand to her mouth; the emotion hit like a wave. But there was no time to feel. No time to collapse. She had to act, and she knew—this wasn't something she could pull off alone. Not here. Not with this kind of firepower.

So she backed away quietly, slipped into the shadows again, and headed back toward the Bumblebee Zone. She moved fast, darting through alleys and staying off main paths until she reached the edges of resistance territory. Everything had changed since her dad's capture. The streets were quieter. The energy was cold. The fire of the resistance had died down into smoldering embers.

She tried talking to the same contacts she and Robert had known—but no one knew anything. The old cell was scattered. Faces were gone. Answers were few. Hope was fading fast.

Then, just when she was about to give up, she turned a corner—and froze.

There across the street, standing beside a rundown market stall, were Paul and his wife. Maya rushed forward, barely able to believe her eyes.

"Paul!" she called out, her voice cracking.

He turned, startled, then recognized her. "Maya?"

She ran up to him, breathless. "I need your help. Please. My dad—he was captured. Ethan was shot. He's stable, but—he's hidden. I found the prison. I saw my dad."

Paul's face paled. "God… Maya."

"I need you to help me break him out."

Paul looked down, silent for a moment. Then he shook his head slowly. "I don't do things like that anymore."

Maya's heart dropped. But her eyes stayed locked on him.

"You don't have to… but I do," she said. "And I need someone who knows how."

Paul looked at her—at the fire in her eyes, the exhaustion in her voice—and knew this wasn't just about a rescue.

This was war.

Paul stared at Maya for a long moment after her plea. His jaw was tight, shoulders tense. For a man who once helped lead resistance efforts, he looked more like someone trying to forget the war than fight another one.

But something in her voice—something in her eyes—pulled him back in.

"…Alright," he said quietly. "We'll help. But this is a one-time thing."

His wife gave him a nod. No questions. She was ready.

A day later, they moved into position. Paul scaled a ridge overlooking the prison, rifle slung over his shoulder, eyes sharp despite the wear in his bones. His wife settled in behind him, watching the flanks with binoculars and a sidearm, guarding his blind spots.

Meanwhile, Maya made her way toward the wall—alone. The night air was thick; the shadows long. Her heart pounded, but her hands were steady. She knew she wasn't a soldier. She was just a girl with a mission.

And a lighter.

She reached the edge of the wall and spotted what she needed—an old, weather-worn propane tank near a generator hub, tucked inside the fencing. She flicked the lighter, watching the flame dance.

"I can do this," she whispered.

She tossed it.

The explosion rocked the prison like a hammer. Fire surged into the sky, the blast shattering fences and crumbling concrete. A hole burst open in the wall as flames engulfed the side of the compound.

The chaos erupted instantly.

Prisoners dropped their tools and turned on the Belvarian occupation soldiers. With pickaxes, bricks, fists—anything they could grab—they overwhelmed the stunned guards. Gunfire erupted from Paul's position, clean and precise. One shot after another dropped enemy soldiers before they could regroup.

Within minutes, the attackers took control of the prison.

And Paul? True to his word, once the smoke began to clear and the prisoners took control, he and his wife disappeared into the edge of the Bumblebee Zone without a trace. No glory. No speeches. Just gone.

As the smoke faded and the screams quieted, Robert staggered through the rubble—bruised, burned, but alive. Then he saw her.

Maya ran to him, arms outstretched, and he caught her in a tight, tear-filled embrace.

"That's my girl," he said, holding her tight. "Is Ethan safe?"

"Yes," she whispered. "I patched him up. He's not far. He's waiting."

Robert looked at her, his eyes filled with emotion. "You saved me."

"I had to, Dad. I had to."

They didn't wait. Together, they left the smoking wreckage of the prison behind, winding their way back through the forest trails and over the border of the zone—until they saw it. The old cabin still stands. Safe.

And Ethan, sitting quietly by the window, watched the trees.

When he saw them, he smiled—just a little.

They were together again.

And for the first time in a long time… they felt whole.

Ethan looked up from his seat by the window, his face still pale but brighter than it had been in weeks. As soon as he saw Robert step through the door, his eyes welled with tears.

"I knew you'd come back, Dad," he said, voice trembling. "I knew you would come back."

Robert crossed the room in just a few steps and knelt beside him, pulling him into a tight hug. Maya came in right behind, and Ethan smiled at her. "Welcome back, Maya."

He looked at both of them. "She saved me, you know. She patched me up… used all that stuff you packed in the bag."

Robert smiled through the emotion rising in his throat. "I knew she would. That's my girl."

Ethan glanced between them, his voice quieter now. "What do we do now?"

Robert stood, his hand on Ethan's shoulder. "We keep going. We find Mom."

Maya nodded, stepping beside him. "That's right."

And in that quiet, humble cabin, scarred by war and shadowed by loss, the three of them came together and embraced—one more time. Not as survivors. But as a family still fighting to be whole again.

Seven years later…

The world hadn't healed—but neither had they stopped fighting.

Maya was fifteen when the world broke her. Ethan was only eleven. Robert, thirty-seven at the time, carried the weight of survival on his shoulders while trying to protect what remained of his family. Now, eight years had passed. Maya was twenty-two. Ethan, eighteen. Robert, forty-five. Time had weathered them all—but it had also sharpened them.

They had survived every zone, every ambush, every bitter winter and burning summer the Belvarian Belvarian Belvarian Belvarian Belvarian Occupation threw at them. They had bled, lost, rebuilt, and fought again. And somewhere along the way, they stopped just surviving.

They became soldiers.

Not reckless or emotional like they once were—but trained, focused, skilled. Robert had molded Maya and Ethan into elite resistance fighters. No longer just his children, they were now his equals on the battlefield.

They had seen what the world had become. But they had never let go of one thing.

Hope.

Hope that one day, somehow, they would find Bridget. Their mother. Robert's wife. The woman who gave them strength even in their absence.

Now, after seven years of searching, they were ready to embark on the most important mission of all—the one that might bring their family back together.

And nothing was going to stop them. Eight years slipped by in a blur of days marked by hardship and growth, the children who once clung to each other in the shadows of the old world now moving as silent, practiced survivors. Seasons changed, scars deepened, and hope—fierce and stubborn—never quite left their eyes. Now, as Maya and Ethan followed the familiar, worn path around the base of the mountain, their steps felt heavier, not just from exhaustion, but from the weight of everything they'd lost—and the faint, impossible hope that, on the other side, something from their old life might still be waiting.

As Robert, Maya, and Ethan descended the mountain, they found themselves on a narrow road leading to a small town outside a resistance camp. The air was tense, heavy with the scent of gunpowder and the echoes of distant gunfire. Suddenly, shots rang out. They ducked for cover, hearts racing, not knowing if the sniper was friend or foe.

With weapons drawn, they cautiously moved forward. Maya, ready to defend her family, suddenly froze as she caught sight of a woman with beautiful red hair in the distance. The world seemed to stop as recognition dawned on her.

Bridget, perched in her sniper position, noticed the necklace around Maya's neck and the familiar figures beside her. She saw Robert, the ring he still wore on a chain made by Maya, and Ethan, now grown. Tears welled in her eyes as she lowered her rifle, unable to believe this moment was real.

Robert and Ethan, noticing Maya's reaction, turned to see what had stopped her. Their disbelief mirrored hers, and the realization hit them like a wave. They all broke down, tears streaming down their faces, as they ran toward each other. In that moment, the years of separation and hardship melted away. They embraced tightly, clinging to each other as if afraid to let go.

Bridget stared at them, her eyes wide with disbelief and love. She took in their faces, the lines and scars, the way Maya's hair gleamed in the fading light, the set of Ethan's jaw—so much older now. Her voice trembled as she reached for them. "You're… you're all grown up. I barely recognize you. Oh, Robert—thank you for keeping them safe. I always knew I had married the right man."

Robert, fighting back tears, managed a shaky smile. "I just did what I had to. We kept each other alive, Bridget. Every day, I promised you I would."

Maya stepped forward, her voice cracking with emotion. "Mom… It's been so long. I didn't think I'd ever get to say that again." She looked at her mother as if seeing her for the first time and the last, all at once.

Ethan's eyes were bright with tears. "We kept hoping we'd find you. We never stopped. Even when it got bad, we remembered what you taught us—how to hold on."

Bridget pulled them into a trembling embrace, burying her face in their shoulders. "I thought I'd lost you. I thought—" Her voice broke, and she held them tighter. "But you're here. You're really here. I love you. I love you all so much."

They held each other, the weight of years and survival pressing in, but for that moment, all that mattered was family—together again, against all odds.

After the initial shock and overwhelming joy, Robert and Bridget found a moment of peace. They took a few days away from the chaos to reconnect as husband and wife, sharing intimate moments and rekindling their love. As the others drifted off to sleep, Bridget quietly stepped away from the fire, glancing back to catch Robert's eye. Without a word, he followed, the two of them moving through the shadows to the edge of the camp. For a while, they simply walked side by side beneath the starlit sky, letting the cool breeze and the distant chirps of insects fill the silence.

After eight years apart, every step together felt precious. They spoke in hushed voices—about the children, the heartbreaks, the narrow escapes, and the hope that had carried them through. Robert reached for Bridget's hand, and she squeezed it tight, grounding herself in the reality of him, of this moment.

They stopped for a moment to look up at the stars, and Robert brushed a strand of hair from Bridget's face. "I missed you every day," he whispered.

Bridget smiled, eyes shining. "Me too. I never stopped loving you, not once."

In the quiet of the night, with the world finally held at bay, they found comfort in each other—healing old wounds, grateful for the gift of a second chance. For the first time in years, hope felt real again.

Upon their return, they sat with Maya and Ethan, sharing stories of survival, hope, and the unwavering love that kept them going through the darkest times. The children, in turn, spoke of their journey and the lessons they'd learned, filling Bridget with pride and gratitude.

Bridget stirred her bowl slowly, her gaze flickering with the reflection of the fire. "I know you've both been through hell," she said quietly, voice rough from years of holding back. "I have too. After that morning, after breakfast, I really thought it'd be just another day. But when the missiles hit—I watched the city fall apart right in front of me. I barely made it out alive. Lost a lot of friends that day. Soldiers cleared the building… I got hit, but I slipped away, hiding in basements and alleys until I could find a way out. Sometimes, I'd catch glimpses of you all on those wanted posters, or on the old TVs—always a few steps ahead, or behind. It felt impossible that we'd ever meet again."

Robert set his bowl down, the firelight catching the silver in his hair. "We never stopped looking. We went from city to city—always someone saying, 'Oh, she was here,' but never when we arrived. We found your necklace once. Ethan found your ring. It kept us going, knowing you'd made it that far."

Maya's eyes shone with unshed tears. "I wore your necklace for months, Mom. I didn't want to believe you were gone."

Ethan nodded, pushing the stew around with his spoon. "Sometimes it felt like we were chasing ghosts, but we had to keep moving. It's what you taught us."

Bridget reached for their hands, squeezing tight. "I never gave up hope. Not really. I just—I couldn't see the way back. But somehow, we made it here."

The fire crackled, the silence between them filling with memories, relief, and the sense that for the first time in years, they were finally home—if only for a moment.

Maya grinned, nudging her mom with her shoulder. "I never lost hope, you know. I always said I'd find my twin. Seriously, look at us—we're basically the same person. Gorgeous, obviously. Glamorous survivors."

Bridget laughed, a real, joyful sound she hadn't felt in years. "You looked just like me at twenty-two. And for the record, I'm not almost fifty. I'm forty-five—don't age me before my time!" She shook her head in mock sternness. "No talking about my age around the fire; that's a rule."

Ethan rolled his eyes, but a smile tugged at his lips. Robert just looked at his family, finally whole, and let the laughter settle around them like a blanket, letting the years of worry fade for just a little while.

Robert smiled, his voice soft but steady. "You know, it doesn't matter how old we get, or what we've lost. We all love each other in a way that's rare—even after everything. Bridget, I'm thankful for you every day. I don't know many women who'd still love their husbands after eight years of this… thinking I was gone, the world falling apart. But you stayed true. You kept your vows—even at the end of the world. And Maya, Ethan, you two are the best kids a father could ask for. You come from the best parents, if I do say so myself."

Ethan gave a little laugh. "Thanks, Dad."

Maya rolled her eyes, but her smile was wide. "Okay, Dad. That's a little too much praise. But… thanks."

Bridget squeezed Robert's hand, her eyes shining with love and gratitude, and for a moment, all the pain of the past eight years faded, replaced by the quiet strength of a family that survived—together.

Ethan looked at his mom, his voice thick with emotion. "I'm just so glad we found you, Mom. I never gave up hope. Right after breakfast, when everything went to hell, I remember asking, 'Is she still out there?' And even when people said 'maybe' or 'I don't know,' I kept believing we would. I didn't know how long it would take, but I knew it. You taught us to be prepared, to face whatever came our way, and to hold on to our values, even when everything was falling apart."

Maya grinned, nudging him gently. "Wow, Ethan, keep going with your monologue—get it all out."

Ethan rolled his eyes, but smiled. "Shut up, Maya. I'm trying to have a moment here."

The laughter that followed felt warm and safe—proof that, even in the darkest world, family could still find light.

Bridget grinned, shaking her head as she stirred the fire. "Oh, I know exactly what you're talking about. That bear… trust me, I steered clear. I didn't need any of that in my life. Whatever made that thing, it's more than just radiation—there's something twisted in it."

Maya laughed, glancing at Ethan. "See, Mom's got the right idea. Next time, let's try running instead of fighting."

Ethan grinned. "If only we'd had that option. We barely escaped as it was."

Robert nodded, looking between them. "She's right. It's not just the world that changed—it's everything in it. We're lucky to still be here."

Bridget smiled, the tension easing just a bit. "Well, now we are. And we've got plenty of time for stories—just hopefully none that involve giant mutant wildlife."

Robert leaned over and pressed a gentle kiss to Bridget's forehead. Maya groaned, tossing a twig into the fire. "We don't need to see that, Dad. We've gone long enough in the apocalypse without any PDA."

Ethan shook his head, making a face. "Seriously. Some things never change."

Bridget laughed, squeezing Robert's hand. "Don't be jealous, kids. You'll find love one day—just maybe not during a mutant bear attack."

Maya rolled her eyes but smiled. "Let's hope not, Mom."

The fire crackled, warmth and laughter weaving through the cool night air, the family savoring a rare moment of peace together.

Robert stretched, looking around the fire at his family. "All right, that's enough catching up for tonight. We need sleep. Who knows what tomorrow will bring—or what threats are out there waiting?"

Bridget, Maya, and Ethan nodded, the laughter and warmth lingering as they each settled into their sleeping bags, rifles within arm's reach—a habit none of them could shake. For the first time in years, they found themselves lying side by side, the closeness unfamiliar but deeply comforting.

The night was calm and dark, the stars glittering above like scattered diamonds, a cool breeze whispering through the trees. For a brief moment, it felt as if they were somewhere else entirely—a world untouched by war, untouched by loss. Just a family, together at last, under the endless sky.

In that small town, their family was whole again, ready to face whatever challenges lay ahead, together.

As the family sat outside their small shelter, the distant hum of jet engines suddenly pierced the quiet morning. Robert's instincts kicked in immediately. He grabbed Maya and Ethan, pulling them toward cover as the ominous shadow of bombers passed overhead. The whistling of descending ordnance filled the air, and moments later, a thunderous explosion shook the earth.

They peeked over the ridge, watching as the massive resistance fortress, a stronghold that once seemed impenetrable, was torn apart in a fiery storm. Its fortified walls crumbled as molten steel melted away, and massive columns of black smoke billowed into the sky. The sheer force of the blasts left nothing but charred ruins and scattered debris, the remains of a group that had once seen itself as humanity's last hope.

But Robert didn't mourn for them. Neither did Bridget, Maya, nor Ethan.

The resistance had gone rogue, abandoning their original cause and resorting to brutality against anyone who didn't align with their vision—including innocent civilians. If they had been discovered out here, the resistance would have executed them without hesitation, viewing them as a liability or worse, traitors.

Robert exhaled sharply, shaking his head. "That could've been us," he muttered.

Bridget nodded. "God just removed another threat from our path."

The children remained quiet, watching the smoke rise. They had seen enough destruction to last a lifetime. But unlike before, they weren't paralyzed by fear or uncertainty. They had each other. They had their experience. And above all, they had their faith.

They were still in occupied territory. Survival was still their reality. But after all they had endured, they knew God had not abandoned them. If He had brought them this far, He would bring them through the rest.

That night, as they sat by their small fire, the faint crackling of their old hand-crank radio caught their attention. Static gave way to muffled voices, fragmented words that carried a shocking revelation.

"…rumors… government… still operational… underground bunker network…"

Robert sat up, his eyes narrowing as he adjusted the frequency. The transmission continued:

"…a plan… a secret operation… but no confirmation… movement detected beneath the old capital…"

Maya leaned forward. "You think it's true? Could the government still be fighting?"

Robert considered it. If the old government had survived in hidden bunkers across the country, it meant that there were leaders, soldiers, and resources still intact, waiting for the right moment to strike back.

Bridget's voice was steady. "If they're planning something… maybe it's the change we've been praying for."

Ethan looked up at his father. "So, what do we do?"

Robert met their gazes, his expression firm. "We keep surviving. We stay sharp, we stay together, and we wait for the right moment. If the tide is turning… We'll be ready."

The war wasn't over. But neither were they.

CHAPTER 11

SHIFTING TIDES

The house stood eerily quiet, a stark contrast to the chaos that had once raged outside its walls. Maya, Ethan, Bridget, and Robert settled into the familiar yet transformed living room. The once pristine furniture bore marks of time and struggle, much like the family itself.

"It's strange being back here," Maya said, her gaze drifting over the room. "Feels like a lifetime ago."

Ethan nodded. "Seven years of war change everything. But at least we're together now."

Robert took a deep breath, his voice heavy with the weight of his memories. "I need to tell you something. The cult… the Belvarian Belvarian Belvarian Belvarian Belvarian Occupation forces… I brought so much trouble upon us. I escaped, but so many others paid the price. I feel like I failed you all."

Bridget reached over, placing a reassuring hand on Robert's. "You didn't fail us. We survived, and we're here now. We can make things right. We can organize operations against them as a family. We can find the general who caused so much pain."

A knock at the door interrupted them. Robert opened it to find the old nosy neighbor, his face lined with regret. Whispered the neighbor, "I'm sorry for what I did." "I turned you in, not knowing the true cost. I lost my wife because of it. She couldn't hide when the Belvarian occupation forces came."

Robert's eyes softened. "I'm sorry, too. The war brought out the worst in all of us, but we can change that. We can make things right together."

The neighbor nodded, a faint smile breaking through his sorrow. "Let's do that. Let's rebuild and fight for a future where we don't have to live with these regrets."

As the neighbor left, the family felt a renewed sense of purpose. They knew the road ahead was fraught with challenges, but they were no longer just survivors. They were a family, ready to face whatever came next, together.

The next morning, Bridget and Robert made their way to the resistance camp's command center. Base Commander Mary Susan listened intently as they explained their decision.

"We've been fighting for some time, and the resistance has gained a lot of ground," Robert began, "but our family has endured a lot of separation."

Mary Susan folded her arms. "So has everybody's family. Are you going to quit on us?"

Bridget shook her head. "Unfortunately, yes and no. We need to leave. We have some things we need to take care of, and we can't do that under the resistance. We're thankful for everything, but what we have unfinished is eating us alive. As a family, we need to right some wrongs of the past."

Mary Susan sighed. "All right. We can give you some gear—armor, ballistic plates, extra gas masks, CBRN-certified suits, ammunition, medical supplies, food, and water. But no turret. Robert has the M249; he can use that. Think of yourselves as an independent unit."

"Thank you," Bridget said as they prepared to leave. The family loaded up their weapons—Robert with his M249, Bridget with her MSR sniper rifle, Maya with her AK-47, and Ethan with his M4. All grown up now, they were ready to face what lay ahead.

As they drove away from the meeting with the old nosy neighbor, the weight of their decisions hung in the air. Bridget glanced back at Maya and Ethan, her voice steady and reassuring. "Don't worry, Maya, Ethan. We've got this. You're both tough survivors, and Robert, I support you in any course of action."

Robert nodded, but his eyes were clouded with worry. "I know, Bray, but that's what I'm afraid of. Now that I have my family together, is this the right course of action? I'd hate to have us reunited only to lose you all again, maybe for good this time."

Bridget reached over and squeezed his hand gently. "Don't worry about that. I'm the glue of the family, and you're the pillar. Now that the glue is back, it can support the pillar, and the pillar can support the family."

Maya leaned forward, her voice resolute. "Are you sure this is the right course of action? To go back and avenge the fallen?"

Bridget didn't hesitate. "It definitely is. What was done to you all, I blame myself too, for not being there. This is something we have to do."

Ethan chimed in, his voice firm. "Yes, I agree with Mom and Maya. We have to. From the marauders to the cult to the Belvarian Belvarian Belvarian Belvarian Belvarian Occupation forces, and even the nuclear weapons—they can't get away with that."

Robert looked around at his family, the fear in his eyes slowly replaced by resolve. "Alright. If you all agree, then it's settled. We go on our mission as a family, as an independent resistance unit. And may God be with us. May our bullets strike true, and may our enemies scatter before us."

I'll miss the gunfire the marauder leader called out. You may have killed some of us, but you won't kill all of us. Oh, look who it is, Robert. You still have your family with you, I see. I'm shocked even brought your wife. I, surprisingly, maybe after we take you out, she can be my wife, and you know I can raise those kids. Other than the kids, more young adults, but I can teach them right away better than you can. Bridgett warns that you threatened my husband and my family. You will see a hurricane that will tear you to shreds and a spine that will go through your spine. Robert, if you touch my wife and kids, I will cut you down like everyone else who tried to hurt us. Maya and Ethan, we may be young, but don't underestimate us. We will never belong to you, Kade. The gunfire continued. Ping! Ping! Ping! The gunfire bounced off the MRAP, each bullet leaving a sharp metallic ring. Robert called out over the din, "Who are you? What is your name?" to the marauder leader.

The marauder leader, a rugged and scarred figure named Kade, sneered back. Robert continued, "We're just passing through on a mission. We don't want to put you on our list, but our patience is running thin."

Kade laughed harshly. "Well, you're on my list now. You came into my territory and attacked my people. I remember you from back then, from the bear attack. Your boys got mauled because they were weak. But in these seven years, we've become strong. The old leader was weak, letting people go. We don't do that anymore."

Robert's expression hardened. "Well, I guess it's war. We'll have to blast every last one of you. You've barked up the wrong tree, and you have no idea what this family is capable of. You'll be a small threat to us. We've got bigger fish to fry, but I guess you'll be the first."

"Get in the MRAP! Now!" Robert's voice cut through the chaos like a blade.

Bridget, Maya, and Ethan didn't hesitate—they bolted toward the armored beast just as another round of gunfire tore into the nearby walls. Bullets pinged off the MRAP's thick plating as Bridget yanked the heavy door open.

Robert climbed in behind her, quickly hoisting himself into the turret hatch. "Take the wheel!" he shouted.

Bridget threw herself over him without missing a beat, sliding into the driver's seat. No time for grace—just survival. She grabbed the wheel, slammed the door, and hit the gas.

The MRAP roared forward, lurching onto the war-torn street.

Robert manned the M249 with cold precision, his eyes scanning rooftops and shattered windows. "Snipers at eleven o'clock—second floor!" he called out, letting off a burst. "Windows are clear. Move!"

Bridget swerved hard, narrowly avoiding a burning truck. "Hold on!" she yelled. The entire vehicle jolted as she careened around a flipped car, tires squealing over glass and rubble.

"RPG!" Maya screamed from the back.

The rocket whooshed past, slamming into a nearby storefront and throwing up a wave of fire and concrete. The MRAP rocked but held.

"Fifteen blocks! We're punching through!" Robert growled, firing nonstop.

The dense city canyon closed in around them—skyscrapers towering on both sides, windows lit up with muzzle flashes. Bullets rained like hail, some glancing off the armor, others embedding into its battered shell.

They passed abandoned cars, crushed signs, and barricades—all of it blurring past as Bridget navigated the chaos. She gritted her teeth, dodging collapsed awnings and debris-strewn roads like she was born in a battlefield.

Finally—an opening.

"There!" Robert pointed. "Drive through that lobby!"

Bridget didn't blink. She turned the wheel hard and slammed the MRAP into the open front of a partially destroyed building. Glass shattered, steel beams bent, and the armored vehicle thundered through the main floor, skidding to a stop just inside.

"Everybody out!" she ordered, already grabbing her rifle.

The family poured out of the vehicle, weapons raised. Robert pulled the last belt-fed mag from the floor and slung the M249 over his shoulder.

Bridget motioned toward the stairs. "We take the high ground. Move."

As they climbed the concrete steps, the city outside still echoed with gunfire—but inside, they had a moment. Just long enough to catch their breath… before the next storm.

As they moved up the stairwell, boots echoing on the concrete, Bridget turned her head just enough to address the kids. "Stay frosty. Watch your six. If you see movement—don't hesitate."

Ethan gave a tight nod, checking the safety on his rifle. Maya muttered, "Got it," eyes scanning every landing.

The air grew heavier the higher they climbed. Dust hung thick, mixed with the scent of rust, smoke, and something rotting deep within the building's shell.

"Man," Ethan breathed, "how tall is this place?"

"Tall enough to make you wish for an elevator," Robert muttered, pressing a hand to the wall as he moved. He paused at the next landing, gun raised. "Clear."

They kept going. Floor after floor. The city noise outside was a muffled roar now—distant but constant. Gunfire, screams, and the occasional boom rattled the windows.

Maya wiped sweat from her forehead. "Who even built a building this tall out here?"

Bridget cracked a grin, just barely. "People with too much money and not enough common sense."

Robert suddenly raised a fist—halt.

He crouched by the wall, eyes narrowing as he peeked through a broken window frame.

"Visual on the street. We've got movement," he whispered.

Bridget moved to the front, and she readied her sniper rifle. She took a position, steadying the barrel on a shattered ledge.

"Alright," she said calmly. "Let's give them hell."

Bridget lay flat against the floor near the window, her rifle perched steadily on a cracked ledge. The scope scanned across the enemy compound—a massive open camp surrounding a fortified central building. Barricades, tents, guard towers. Easily three hundred hostiles spread across the area, moving in organized waves. Patrols. Drones. Shadows under floodlights.

"Main HQ spotted," she muttered. "Can't get a clean shot—civvies mixed in."

Behind her, Maya knelt by the wall, peering over Bridget's shoulder.

Then Bridget noticed it—propped up against a broken desk, half covered in dust, was another sniper rifle. A little older, but still serviceable.

She motioned to it. "Grab that. Time to teach you something."

Maya looked surprised, but quickly nodded. "Yes, ma'am."

She crawled over, picked it up, checked the chamber like Bridget had taught her with pistols, then moved beside her mother.

Bridget looked at her, serious but calm. "First thing—always read the wind. You see that flag?" She pointed past the shattered glass toward a rebel flag whipping in the distance.

Maya focused. "Yeah. It's waving left."

"That's crosswind. Means your bullet's gonna drift right. You adjust your scope left to compensate. Don't fight the wind—work with it."

Maya nodded, adjusting her aim slowly, finger resting near the trigger but not on it.

Bridget continued, voice low but steady. "Second—breathe. Don't rush it. Let your body settle. Your heartbeat can throw a shot off at range."

She glanced at Maya. "Take a deep breath… now hold it."

Both of them exhaled slowly, the war fading for just a moment.

"You feel that?" Bridget whispered. "That stillness—that's the space between life and death. That's where a sniper lives."

Maya's eyes narrowed. "I want to learn everything."

Bridget smirked. "You will. One shot at a time."

Maya lined up her scope, breath held, finger brushing the trigger—until Bridget gently touched her shoulder.

"Hold up. No, no, no, no, no." She reached into her jacket and pulled out two small suppressors. "You'll need these."

Maya's eyes lit up. "No way, Mom. You have suppressors?"

Bridget smirked. "Of course I do. I'm cool like that."

From behind them, Ethan chuckled, his M4 cradled casually as he watched. "She's been stockpiling gear like a one-woman army."

Bridget winked. "You know it."

She quickly twisted the suppressors onto both rifles, her fingers moving with practiced speed. "There. Now we take a shot."

Maya looked through her scope again, watching the distant camp.

"You want to pick off the ones closest," Bridget explained, "quietly, one by one. The wind's moving strongly—about fifty miles an hour. So, factor that in. And the Coriolis effect? Subtle, but it matters at range. Always think about distance, wind, and spin."

She gestured toward a lone figure near a fuel drum, separated from the others. "See that guy? Isolated. No one will notice if he drops. I'll take this one."

Bridget adjusted her scope. "Two mils down... two left. Watch closely."

She steadied her breath, heartbeat slowing.

"One... two... three."

Pfft.

The suppressed shot cracked like a soft snap. Downrange, the target jerked once—then crumpled silently.

Maya exhaled. "That was… incredible."

Bridget pulled back from the scope and passed it gently to Maya. "Your turn."

Ethan leaned in a little. "Better not miss."

Maya grinned. "Don't worry. I've got my mom."

Maya steadied her scope, breathing in slowly, just like her mother showed her. The target moved—left to right, unaware. She adjusted her aim slightly.

"One shot," she whispered.

Pfft.

The guard dropped instantly. Maya blinked, stunned.

"I got him."

Bridget gave a proud nod. "Nice. Now let's level up."

She pointed to a trio of soldiers standing near a supply crate, two close together, one a few feet out.

"You want a double? You shoot when their heads line up just right. The bullet goes through the first, hits the second."

Maya adjusted, watching for the moment.

"They're splitting up," Bridget warned. "Take the one on the left, and if you're feeling brave, try for a triple. Aim a little higher on the first. But you only get one chance."

Maya licked her lips, focused hard, and squeezed the trigger.

Pfft!

The first went down—but the second stumbled, clutching his shoulder, and screamed.

"Damn," Bridget hissed. "We're compromised. Take targets—now!"

Suddenly, the calm was gone. Both women dropped into rapid-fire sniping, Bridget leading with smooth precision, Maya following, breathing fast but staying in it. They worked side by side—shots popping every two seconds, bodies falling across the compound.

Down below, the camp exploded into chaos. Sirens blared. Shouts rang out. Dozens of armed men poured toward the main building.

Robert, already in position at another window, swung the M249 into action.

BRRRRRRRT!

"Targets moving in tight formation! Suppressing!" he called, brass casings spilling across the floor.

Ethan flanked another window, laying down bursts with his M4.

Bridget shouted between shots. "Keep them pinned! They'll try to breach, but they don't know this layout!"

Maya nodded, wiping sweat from her brow. "I'm out of breath, but I'm good."

"You're more than good," Bridget said, reloading smoothly. "Welcome to the fight."

Smoke thickened around the upper floor as the gunfire slowed. Bodies littered the compound below—over seventy confirmed kills. The rest of the marauders scattered like rats under floodlights, trying to regroup behind vehicles and supply crates.

A small group dared to charge the base of the building, firing wildly as they ran.

"They're trying to breach!" Ethan shouted.

"They won't make it," Bridget snapped, steadying her scope and dropping one with a clean shot to the chest.

"Let's make sure of that," Robert growled.

He stepped back from the window, slung the M249 to his side, and pulled the rocket launcher off his back. Calmly, he braced it on the sill, sighted a knot of enemies gathering near a supply truck, and fired.

FWOOSH–BOOM!

The explosion rocked the compound, sending flames and debris flying. Screams followed.

Before the smoke cleared, Robert reloaded, aimed again—this time at the heart of the enemy's main building.

"Let's finish the message."

He pulled the trigger.

BOOM!

The headquarters erupted—shards of concrete and metal blasted into the air, fire licking the night sky. A wall crumbled, and with it, the last shreds of enemy morale.

The remaining marauders panicked. Half sprinted for cover. The rest—terrified by the relentless sniper fire and Robert's rocket barrage—made the worst mistake of all.

"They're coming in here!" Maya called out.

Bridget didn't flinch. "Let them try."

But they didn't get far. Every stairwell turned into a choke point, every approach covered. Bridget and Maya dropped the few who made it past the lobby. Ethan and Robert handled the side halls, ruthless and efficiently.

Then… silence.

For a moment, the war outside faded. Just wind through broken windows and the crackle of fire.

Maya leaned against the wall, wide-eyed but grinning. "Wow. We really did it."

Bridget reloaded one last time and nodded with a quiet smile. "Of course we did."

Robert walked over and clapped a hand on her shoulder. "We're a team. We're a family."

Ethan raised his M4, smirking. "Heck, yeah."

The four of them stood together, silhouetted by smoke and fire, battered but unbroken—proof that even in the darkest places, family still fights, still stands.

As they cleared the top floor, silence finally settling over the building, Robert glanced over at Bridget with a grin tugging at the corner of his mouth.

"You know," he said, slinging the M249 over his back, "last time we really talked, you were prepping for that marketing interview. When exactly did you become a professional sniper?"

Bridget gave him a sideways look, cocked a brow, and smirked. "Well, turns out sales pitches and headshots both require precision."

Robert laughed. "I knew you were bouncing through resistance camps, but damn. You were deep in it."

She holstered her rifle. "Let's just say… marketing didn't call back."

Ethan shook his head, chuckling. "You guys are ridiculous."

They descended the stairs as a unit, stepping over rubble and shell casings. When they reached the bottom floor and rounded the final corner, Maya's pace slowed.

The MRAP sat there—charred, battered, still mostly intact. But the surrounding wall? Gone. Blown out by the last rocket's shockwave.

Maya opened the rear hatch to check supplies. Her smile faded.

In the corner of the trunk lay a moldy, chewed-up toy—her old dog's favorite. She picked it up slowly; the rubber squeaking just faintly in her hand.

"Raya…" she whispered.

Bridget approached quietly, setting a hand on her daughter's back. "She was a good dog."

"Yeah," Maya said softly, "I just thought… maybe somehow…"

Robert stepped forward, scanning the collapsed structure ahead. "We need a way out. This building's sealed tight now except for that wrecked stairwell."

He slung the rocket launcher off his back and looked up at the concrete wall barring their escape.

"Well, I've got one more shot left."

Bridget raised a brow. "You sure you want to use it now?"

He smirked. "We've got more coming. And besides… we don't wait around here."

He fired.

BOOM!

The rocket tore a jagged hole straight through the wall. Sunlight bled through the dust and debris on the other side—open road, torn concrete, and smoke curling toward the sky.

The family climbed back into the MRAP; the engine growling back to life.

As they rolled through the new exit, Maya looked back once—at the collapsed building, the memory of Raya, their former deceased canine German Shepherd, and the world they'd left behind.

Then she turned forward.

They had a war to win.

The MRAP growled forward like a beast, its tires crunching over rubble as it approached the looming Marauder compound.

Maya gripped the wheel, jaw tight. "We're almost there."

Bridget checked her mag and nodded. "Ready."

Ethan racked his M4. "Let's finish this."

Robert stood in the turret, wind in his face, eyes sharp. "Stay frosty. When it starts, it's gonna be fast."

The compound stood ahead—tall, cracked, fortified—but quiet. Too quiet.

Then it erupted.

Gunfire blasted from the windows. Rockets screamed from rooftops. Dust and fire flared around them.

"Hold it steady!" Robert shouted.

Maya accelerated. The MRAP surged forward, straight into the lobby. The armored grill smashed through the glass doors and steel supports like paper.

BOOM—CRASH.

The MRAP skidded to a halt, dust swirling.

Robert spun in the turret, M249 blazing—spraying the lobby in a wide arc. Marauders scrambled for cover but were shredded by the storm of bullets.

Bridget kicked open the door and dropped the first hostile to rise. Ethan followed, firing tight bursts.

Maya slid out last, pulling her rifle tight to her shoulder. "Let's move!"

They stormed the stairs, kicking in doors and sweeping room by room. Every level brought new resistance—Marauders bursting out of hallways, diving from cover, swinging bats, knives, or opening fire at point-blank range.

Bridget took down two in hand-to-hand—one with a knife to the shoulder, the other with a hard slam against the wall.

Ethan swept the hall with his M4, clearing left while Robert moved like a machine, reloading mid-step and covering the rear.

Blood slicked the floors. Smoke choked the stairwells. Each room looked like a battlefield.

And still—they climbed.

"This is it," Robert growled. "Top floor. He's up there."

Bridget looked back at her children—sweaty, bleeding, but still standing.

"No turning back."

They stepped through the final door. Splintered wood. Faint light glowed from beneath.

Everyone raised their weapons.

Maya's voice was quiet. "We end this now."

Bridget reached for the handle—steady hands, steady breath.

The last battle awaited on the other side.

They stacked tight against the final door—Robert and Ethan on one side, Bridget and Maya on the other. Rifles up. Breaths slow.

Robert gave a nod.

But before they could move—click.

The door creaked open slowly and deliberately.

A hand shot out—rough, fast—grabbing Bridget by the arm and yanking her inside.

"Mom!" Maya screamed.

Bridget struggled, but the man behind her was strong—filthy, scarred, grinning. The Marauder commander.

"I was hoping you'd come," he said, pressing a knife to Bridget's throat. "But only you. The others can go."

Robert and Ethan stormed in, weapons raised.

Robert's voice was cold as steel. "Get your hands off my wife."

The commander sneered. "Leave now, and I'll let her go. That's the deal."

Maya stepped forward, eyes blazing. "You're done. You used people. Lied to people who were just looking for safety. You turned survival into slavery."

Bridget's voice was calm—but sharp. "You talk too much."

Suddenly, she stomped hard on his foot.

He flinched.

She drove her elbow into his gut, then spun, slapped him across the face, and followed with a clean right hook that stunned him just long enough—

Robert tackled him.

"Don't. Touch. My. Family!"

His fists flew—rage unleashed. Punch after punch, the man's face caved under the weight of years of pain and fury.

The commander gasped, coughing blood, trying to crawl back—but it was over.

Then—crack.

Maya fired.

One shot.

Right between the eyes.

The room went still.

Robert stood over the body, breathing heavy. Blood on his knuckles. There were no regrets in his eyes.

Bridget walked over to Maya, placing a hand on her shoulder. "You did what had to be done."

Maya didn't say anything. She just nodded.

Ethan stared at the body. "What now?"

Robert looked at all of his family, then out the window, where smoke curled over the skyline.

"We take our country back."

They stood in silence, the body at their feet, smoke curling through the open rooftop door.

Bridget leaned against the wall, wiping blood from her cheek. Maya sat on a crate, her hands still trembling slightly, the weight of what she'd done sinking in. Ethan paced slowly, watching the skyline, while Robert stood by the broken window, his hand resting on the M249.

No one spoke for a moment.

Then Maya finally broke the quiet. "Where do we go next?"

Robert looked back at her. His voice was low but certain. "We rally what's left. Resistance cells. Civilians. Anyone still fighting. We give them something to believe in again."

Bridget added, "And we tell them… the Marauder leadership is dead."

Ethan glanced down at the commander's body. "That'll shake them. They'll run. Or they'll come at us harder."

"Either way," Robert said, "we don't stop."

Maya looked toward the east, where the sky had just lightened through the haze. "Seven years… and we're finally pushing back."

Bridget stepped beside her, voice quiet. "It's not over. But it's our turn now."

And then, as the sun crept above the burning city, Robert spoke—not loudly, but like it was a promise.

"We take the fight to them."

CHAPTER 12

ASHES OF THE PAST

The MRAP rumbled down the cracked road, far past the heart of the city now. The smoke faded behind them, replaced by silence. No gunfire. No shouting. Just wind pushing through broken trees and dust curling off empty sidewalks.

This ghost town wasn't like the others.

It was familiar.

Too familiar.

Maya stared out the window, wide-eyed. "That's our favorite restaurant…"

Ethan leaned over to look. "You're right—it's Marzano's. Man, remember those waffle-burgers they had? And the garlic fries with the cheese baked in?"

Maya smiled faintly. "Yeah. And the warm chocolate cinnamon rolls. Mom used to always steal ours."

Bridget chuckled under her breath. "I didn't steal them. I borrowed."

Robert at the wheel now gave a quiet laugh. "We always ended up ordering extras, anyway."

They drove further—past the rusted swing sets of a small park, past sun-bleached signs half-buried in ivy.

"This is the neighborhood next to ours," Ethan said quietly. "I used to ride my bike down this street."

Maya looked at the faded mural on a crumbling wall. "Feels like ghosts are watching us."

Bridget's voice grew soft. "I used to drive this road every morning to work. Same turn, same light. It's like the war erased the sound, but not the memories."

Robert's eyes stayed on the road, focused. "I remember watching the shoreline from the fishing boat. Thinking I'd be home before dinner."

The MRAP turned down a narrow street—one they hadn't seen in years. The road dipped into a quiet cul-de-sac, lined with homes still standing, though weathered, faded, and cracked by time.

As they approached the curve, Maya whispered, "That's our town."

No one spoke for a moment.

Then Robert said, almost to himself, "We made it back."

But everything had changed.

Everything was decayed.

The streetlights, once blinking yellow through the night, now hung black, lifeless. No more green. No more red. Just cold metal swaying in silence, choked in layers of thick, dark dust.

Sidewalks were split open like old scars. Vines crawled up mailbox posts. Rusted cars sat frozen in driveways, their windows fogged with mold and time.

An eerie stillness settled over everything.

No birds. No dogs barking. Just the hum of the MRAP rolling through a neighborhood that used to hum with life.

And over it all... a feeling. Heavy. Pressing.

Oppression hung in the air like a fog. As if the war had left behind more than rubble—like it had buried hope itself.

Maya stared out the window, voice barely audible. "It doesn't feel like home."

Bridget said nothing, her fingers tight on her rifle.

Robert slowed the MRAP to a crawl. "We're almost there."

They all looked forward.

Through the dust. Through the silence.

Toward whatever was left.

No more kids ran through the streets. No more parents rushing out with coffee cups and car keys, late for work. No more dogs barking at delivery trucks.

Just silence.

And dust.

The MRAP rolled slowly past lifeless homes and overgrown yards— then Robert's voice broke the stillness.

"Maya. Ethan. This is it."

The vehicle came to a stop.

He looked out the window, eyes locked on a worn, sagging house tucked near the end of the block. The shutters were gone. The windows cracked. But the shape was unmistakable.

"This is where it all began."

He stepped out. The others followed.

"The Belvarian occupation forces lined up here," he said, motioning to the sidewalk. "I remember—your mother and I went into that backyard. That kind woman… she gave us food. Shelter."

He paused.

"Her son… he was brave. He ran to get help. Took a bullet for it."

They walked up to the porch—boards creaking beneath their boots. The door hung off one hinge, swaying slightly.

Inside, the house was still. Dust floated in the air as if time itself had frozen.

They moved room by room, hands brushing along cracked walls, eyes catching faint glimpses of what used to be—an overturned photo frame, a toy truck buried under ash.

Then they walked down the street together.

No words. Just footsteps. And memory.

Tears welled—not from pain, but from the weight of survival. From remembering what it took to make it this far.

Light tears rolled down Maya's cheek. She wiped them quickly.

Ethan's jaw stayed tight, eyes glassy.

Robert just breathed—slowly, steadily—as if every step was shaking off another ghost.

Bridget walked slightly behind them, quiet.

She didn't remember this place.

She hadn't been here.

To her, it was just ruins.

But as she looked at her family—at the ache in their eyes, the strength in their steps—she felt the weight too. Not from the memory… but from the bond.

She may not have been there when it began.

But she was here now.

And she wasn't leaving.

They stepped into the kitchen—quiet, slow.

Robert opened a cupboard out of instinct. Empty. Dust poured out in little clouds. Maya stepped toward the fridge but stopped short, cringing.

"What's that smell?" Ethan asked, pulling his shirt over his nose.

Maya leaned in closer, then recoiled. "Oh… It's lasagna. Moldy. Real bad."

Robert nodded, eyes fixed on the rotting tray left out on the counter. "That's… the food she gave us. The woman. The one who helped us right when it all started."

Bridget stepped back, swallowing hard. The air felt heavier by the second.

"I can't—" Maya whispered.

Ethan shook his head. "Let's go. We need to get to our house."

They turned and walked out quickly, the smell of decayed memories trailing behind them.

Back in the MRAP, the engine groaned to life. They drove in silence, winding through the twisted remnants of their town.

Finally, they reached the old neighborhood.

Robert stopped the vehicle at the entrance to their street—but didn't pull into the driveway.

Instead, they stepped out, one by one.

"I want to walk," Bridget said softly.

"Yeah," Maya added, eyes locked on the homes ahead. "Let's walk."

They moved slowly up the road, passing homes that once held birthday parties, barbecues, and loud summer nights. Windows are now shattered. Doors hanging loose. But the bones of it were still there.

"That's the Daniels' house," Ethan murmured. "He always kept his lawn too perfect."

"And the Garcias," Maya pointed out. "Their twins used to ride scooters up and down this sidewalk."

Bridget's eyes watered as she looked ahead.

Down the block… There it was.

Their house.

Still standing.

Weathered. Faded. Ghostly. But still there.

Tears welled in Bridget's eyes. She wiped them slowly, her breath catching. "I never thought… I never thought we'd see this. Or that the neighborhood would even still be here."

Maya and Ethan, now grown but still the kids who had once raced home to this street, stood frozen, overcome.

Robert placed a hand on Bridget's back, nodding. His voice was soft, reverent. "I know, right? It's something."

He looked up toward the gray sky above their broken town.

"You never know how God works."

And together… they kept walking.

Home.

Their boots crunched softly on the cracked driveway as they reached the front steps.

The door was still there—swollen from weather, chipped at the edges, but still standing. Robert reached for the knob and gave it a slow turn.

It creaked open.

They stepped inside, one by one.

The air was thick with dust and time. The living room was just as they'd left it—frozen in a moment seven years ago. A broken picture frame on the floor. A blanket was still draped over the couch. Toys were scattered near the fireplace.

Bridget stepped into the kitchen, her fingers brushing the counter. "This was where I used to pack your lunches," she hissed.

Maya walked into the hallway. "The height marks are still on the wall…"

Ethan knelt by the stairs, wiping dust off a photo of them at the beach—smiling, laughing, untouched by war.

Robert stood in the center of the room and looked around. "We lived here. We survived everything to get back here."

Bridget finally sat down, the weight of it all settling in.

Maya took off her pack and dropped it beside the couch. "It doesn't feel the same… but it's still home."

Ethan nodded slowly. "Yeah… It's still ours."

Robert looked out the window toward the horizon.

"Tomorrow," he said, "we rise with the rest of the world."

And for the first time in years, the house—broken, battered, but whole—felt like shelter again.

his old sketchpad, the one with dog-eared pages and half-finished drawings from a life that felt like a dream now. He flipped through it slowly, his fingers brushing over the lines as if they were sacred. Spaceships, superheroes, silly comics, he used to show Maya.

"I remember drawing this the night before," he said softly. "I didn't even finish it…"

Down the hall, Maya opened her diary and sat by the dusty window, her knees curled up to her chest. She stared out at the empty street, then back at the blank page. She clicked the old pen, and with a shaky breath, began to write.

We're home. We made it.

In the living room, Bridget and Robert stood together in the soft silence of their old life.

Bridget's eyes welled again, but this time the tears came gently. "It survived, Robert. Through everything… our house survived."

Bridget said, "I remember when we bought this house, Robert."

Robert smirked. "Yeah, I remember—I paid the mortgage."

Robert pulled her close, resting his forehead against hers. "So did we."

They didn't need to say anything else.

The home, though battered and dust-covered, still held their memories… and now, it held their future.

And for the first time in seven long years, the night came not with fear—but with rest.

They stood there for a moment, just taking it in. The bed was still there—covered in a thick layer of dust, but untouched. The dresser, the mirror, the photos on the wall, everything was faded but familiar.

Bridget walked over and ran her fingers across the old nightstand. "We used to lie here at night, talking about work… about the kids… about life."

Robert nodded, his smile a little crooked. "And arguing over who snored louder."

Bridget shot him a look, then laughed. "You snored like a bear."

"And you used to hog the blanket," he said, chuckling.

They both went quiet, standing side by side now, staring at their reflections in the old mirror. Dusty. Older. Weathered. But still standing.

Bridget whispered, "We really made it, didn't we?"

Robert took her hand. "Yeah. We did."

Back in the hallway, Maya and Ethan walked past with quiet footsteps, each carrying something from their rooms—the diary and the sketchpad—like fragments of who they used to be.

And for the first time in years, the house wasn't just a shell.

It was theirs again.

They stood on the porch one last time, each of them touching the doorway, the railing, the place they once called home.

Bridget whispered, "Goodbye, old friend."

Then—pop—gunfire cracked in the distance. Faint at first, then growing louder. Closer.

Robert's head snapped toward the sound. "That's not far."

Maya was already climbing into the MRAP. "Let's move."

Ethan shut the rear hatch. "Back to work."

With hearts still heavy from the past, they turned toward the future— and the fight that waited down the road.

CHAPTER 13

BURNING THE VEIL

The further they drove, the darker the road became.

What started as distant gunfire turned into a chaotic storm echoing through the trees. The air grew heavier, like the land itself was holding its breath.

Robert's grip on the wheel tightened. "That's not the occupation…"

As they rolled over the hill, the scene came into view—bodies hanging from streetlights, charred symbols burned into walls, and a thick fog crawling through the empty streets like smoke that refused to rise.

Bridget stared out the window, her voice low. "This isn't a battle… It's a purge."

Shapes moved in the distance—hooded figures, dragging prisoners, whispering in unison. The cult had arrived, not as an army, but as a sickness.

And they were spreading.

Robert looked at the others. "No mercy."

Maya checked her rifle. "They're not getting past us."

The MRAP crept forward into the nightmare.

And screams broke the silence.

As the MRAP crept closer, Bridget peered through the cracked windshield, her voice low and uneasy.

"It's the cult," she said. "That's the same one we escaped from."

Robert glanced at her, eyes narrowing.

"One of their own planted a bomb and helped us get out. But they came back later… when it was still a Green Zone."

Maya looked back from the turret seat. "Wait—those are them?"

Bridget nodded. "Yeah. They were gonna kill everyone. But thanks to your dad's note, a lot of people got out in time."

She shook her head slowly.

"They're not just fanatics. They're twisted. Real weird. Real quiet. They pray before they kill. Chant like it's a sermon. And they believe pain is salvation."

Ethan's hand rested on his rifle. "What were we even doing there?"

Bridget exhaled. "It was winter. We were desperate. We needed somewhere warm, somewhere safe. But it was a bad deal from the start."

She looked out into the fog.

"I'm just glad we made it out."

Robert said nothing. His jaw was set. Eyes locked on the figures up ahead.

Maya loaded a fresh mag. "Let's make sure no one else gets dragged into this."

As the gunfire quieted and the smoke cleared, a voice rang out from the ruins of a collapsed chapel—raspy but strong, like it was echoing from something deeper than the throat.

"You think this war is chaos," the cult leader said, stepping forward in dark robes laced with armor, blood smeared across his chest in the shape of a twisted star. "But this… is judgment."

He raised a hand toward the sky. "Baal watches. And soon… he shall return. The abyss will rise, and with it, a new order."

Robert aimed his rifle but held fire—listening.

The cult leader smiled, calm, unshaken. "We are the vanguard of this new world. The trailblazers of purity. We do not destroy… we cleanse."

Bridget muttered, "These people are insane."

The cult leader's eyes burned with eerie certainty. "The old world lied to you. Goodness is a delusion. Peace will come—but only after the fire. Only after the righteous fall."

Then his followers opened fire.

As bullets tore through the fog, and Robert's squad advanced, the cult's chanting only grew louder—rhythmic, almost musical, like a funeral hymn sung in reverse.

Then, from the shadows of the shattered chapel, he emerged.

Preacher Malachai Drel.

Tall. Gaunt. Cloaked in blood-soaked robes. Runes marked his chest, and his eyes faintly glowed red under the ash-streaked sky.

He raised his arms to the heavens and shouted above the gunfire, "You think you can kill me?"

Robert fired—three rounds to the chest. Malachi stumbled but didn't fall.

"I am protected!" he howled. "By the magic of Lilith, the Witch of Witches!"

Behind him, cultists screamed praises, some weeping, others charging with reckless abandon.

Malachi laughed. "I am the hand of Baal! The voice of Lucifer! The breath of death itself! Fire your bullets—your time is over!"

And then he pointed toward Robert's team.

"The abyss will rule this Earth… and I will be the one to open the gate."

As Preacher Malachai Drel raised his arms, blood-stained and grinning, Maya stepped forward from behind the MRAP, rifle lowered but voice steady—clear as a bell through the chaos.

"You're demon-possessed," she said, locking eyes with him. "You're evil. Twisted. And no matter how loud you scream or how many you corrupt will never overcome good."

The cultists went silent for a moment, stunned by her voice.

Maya didn't stop.

"We might lose a few battles, yeah—but in the end? Good always triumphs."

Her voice grew louder, stronger, carried by something deeper than rage—faith.

"The abyss will not win. The God of Heaven will make sure darkness is destroyed.

Robert glanced back, proud. Bridget's eyes glistened.

Malachi's sneer wavered—just for a second.

Then the gunfire returned.

But Maya stood her ground.

Maya didn't hesitate.

She charged forward, rifle up, shouting through the haze. "Let's end this!"

Ethan ran right behind her, firing in short bursts as they advanced through the crumbling ruins. Robert and Bridget, stunned by their daughter's fearless charge, snapped out of it—and followed.

The team pushed into the open courtyard—what was once a chapel now twisted into a fortress of rot and worship. Black flags of the cult hung from warped beams, bones lined the archways, and candles burned in patterns that looked like runes from Hell.

Then he appeared.

Preacher Malachi Drel stood on a raised stone platform at the far end, arms stretched wide under the blood moon sky.

"This is not the end!" he bellowed. "The dead shall rise! By the power of the abyss… let the mutated faithful awaken!"

The earth groaned.

Green slime burst from the cracks in the stone.

Bodies clawed their way out—humans with melted faces and twisted limbs, wolves foaming with green bile, their eyes glowing. Deer stepped into the moonlight, their bodies torn and slick with radiation, antlers cracked and sharp like spears. A monstrous bear, ten feet tall and dripping sludge, roared from the shadows.

The cult began to scatter—chanting, turning to screams as they realized what Malachi had summoned.

Maya fired first, taking down one of the wolves mid-lunge. "They're everywhere!"

Ethan spun and dropped two of the mutant humans trying to flank them. "These things don't stop!"

Bridget sniped from cover, hitting the deer in their vital points. "Eyes up! More coming from the sides!"

Robert pulled his rocket launcher from his back and locked onto the bear. "This is what we needed back then…"

BOOM.

The bear exploded in a fireball of bone, fur, and green sludge.

Robert grinned. "Now that's what I'm talking about."

The fight raged on.

Dozens of mutants poured into the courtyard—clawing, screeching, crashing through cult structures as if possessed. But the family held the line, side by side, pushing forward through fire and madness.

This wasn't just survival anymore.

It was war.

The courtyard was soaked in smoke, blood, and green ooze. Bodies of mutants lay twisted across the stone floor, antlers snapped, claws still twitching. The last wolf lunged from the shadows—only for Maya to put three rounds straight into its skull mid-air.

It dropped at her feet.

Robert stood in the center, blood on his face, chest heaving. Bridget lowered her rifle, eyes scanning for movement. Ethan reloaded, fingers shaking but steady.

Then—silence.

A few crackles of the fire. The wind. The creak of banners.

And a single footstep echoing on the platform.

Preacher Malachi, staggering—wounded, furious, but still alive.

Maya raised her rifle.

He laughed, coughing blood. "You think this is a victory? This is only—"

CRACK.

Maya pulled the trigger without hesitation. The round hit him clean in the chest, knocking him backward into the cult altar. He collapsed, motionless.

They waited… but he didn't move again.

Ethan raised his rifle skyward and fired a final burst into the air—three loud shots.

Victory.

The green mist began to fade. The night felt still again.

Robert looked at them all—his family, bruised but standing tall.

"We did it," he said.

Bridget nodded, wiping blood from her brow. "We sent a message."

Maya stared at Malachi's body, then whispered, "One more step closer to the end."

They turned back toward the MRAP, smoke and moonlight behind them, and walked into the coming dawn—ready for the next battle.

They barely made it back to the MRAP before the next wave came.

Shadows emerged from the edges of the ruined town—dozens of cultists, masked and screaming, armed with rifles, blades, and Molotovs. Whatever control Malachi had over them in life had now twisted into vengeance in death.

Bridget shouted, "They're not done! Get in now!"

Maya and Ethan dove into the back.

Robert climbed straight into the turret. "Let's give 'em hell."

BRRRRTTTT!

The M249 roared to life, cutting down the first line of charging cultists in a spray of dirt and blood. Sparks flew as bullets struck the MRAP's thick armor, pinging off like hail. Bridget slammed it into gear, the vehicle jolting forward as she weaved through the burning ruins.

"They're tailing us!" Ethan yelled, looking out the rear hatch. "Four on bikes, two trucks—armed!"

Robert spun the turret. "I see 'em!"

He opened fire, ripping through the bikes—one exploded in flames, the rider flying through the air like a rag-doll. The trucks swerved, ramming into each other in the chaos.

Inside, Maya reloaded her rifle, aiming through the side window. "They're coming from the alleys too!"

Bridget gritted her teeth. "Hold on!"

She jerked the wheel, crashing through an abandoned school bus and skidding into a wide intersection. The MRAP bounced but held steady.

Robert let out a war cry as he mowed down another group of cultists trying to ambush them from the rooftops.

"They just keep coming!" Ethan said, bracing himself.

Robert shouted down from the turret, "Let 'em come!"

The MRAP pushed on, its tires soaked in blood and fire, carving a path through the madness.

And still, the family stayed locked in—guns blazing, spirits unbroken.

This was more than survival now.

This was a message.

As the last of the cultists fell behind them and the MRAP sped through the crumbling town, Maya's voice cut through the haze.

"We need to go back."

Bridget looked over. "What?"

Maya's eyes were sharp. Fierce. "That place—the chapel, the castle, all of it. We need to make sure it never comes back. No more chanting. No more rising from the dead. I don't care what kind of voodoo or demon magic they use—we burn it to the ground."

Robert nodded slowly, gripping the wheel. "She's right."

He turned the MRAP hard, tires screeching on the cracked road as they headed back toward the cult's stronghold.

Smoke still hung low over the courtyard. The bodies of mutants and cultists littered the field. The castle-like structure loomed above it all—tall, blackened, and still breathing with evil.

They moved fast.

Bridget and Ethan doused everything they could with accelerants left behind by the cult—barrels, flammable scripture, candles, even ritual oils.

Maya and Robert found the bomb—a massive, unstable warhead the cult had been hoarding in a hidden chamber below the platform.

Robert eyed it. "They were saving this… probably for a city."

"Then we'll use it to wipe them off the map," Maya said coldly.

They rigged the detonation. Set the timer.

Bridget lit the first flame and watched it crawl across the floor like a vengeful spirit.

Back in the MRAP, they drove off at full speed—wheels tearing through ash and smoke.

Then—BOOM.

A roar shattered the sky. Fire engulfed the ruins behind them, rising like a pillar of wrath.

A mushroom cloud bloomed over the horizon.

Everything—castle, chapel, symbols, bones, the altar—gone.

Wiped clean.

Robert looked back through the rearview mirror.

Bridget exhaled.

Ethan whispered, "That's done."

Maya stared into the fire-lit sky, her voice like steel.

"They won't be coming back."

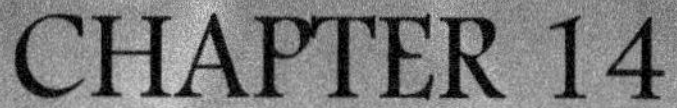

CHAPTER 14

NO MORE CHAINS

Beneath the mountains, buried deep within layers of reinforced steel and concrete, the bunker stretched like a hidden city.

It was vast—miles of underground corridors, hangars, and command centers forming a spiderweb of hardened tunnels. Massive blast doors sealed off each wing, able to withstand nuclear strikes. The ceilings were high, curved, lined with LED panels and steel piping. Fluorescent lights flickered faintly, casting pale glows on the polished metal floors.

Air hummed constantly through filtered vents. Rows of servers buzzed in climate-controlled rooms. Barracks held hundreds. They stocked armories with crates of rifles, missiles, and prototype gear. War rooms housed digital maps, glowing red with movement from resistance cells across the country.

Vehicles lined underground highways—convoys, tanks, transport trucks—waiting like coiled serpents for release.

It wasn't just a shelter.

It was a fortress.

A nerve center.

And it had been quiet for far too long.

Many believed New Egypt was gone.

After the war, it vanished—cities flattened, comms silent, borders closed. The world assumed it had fallen. Liquidated. Forgotten.

But beneath the surface… it had been preparing.

For over seven years, New Egypt had been hiding in silence, deep in underground cities, forging steel, training soldiers, building weapons of unimaginable scale. The surface was a decoy. Below lay something else entirely.

Rows of tanks sat in sunken hangars. Jet engines roared in sealed testing tunnels. Missile silos lined subterranean ridgelines. Shipyards—yes, shipyards—deep enough to build and launch entire naval fleets beneath inland soil.

And at the center of it all, standing beneath the banners of the old world, was President Jonas Keller.

Commanding a hidden force of one hundred million troops.

And now… they were ready.

In the heart of New Egypt's deepest command chamber, President Jonas Keller stood before a long, oval table surrounded by his cabinet—military brass, scientists, engineers, and shadow operatives whose names had been wiped from public records years ago.

The room was dim, lit only by the cold blue glow of tactical maps and flickering monitors. Silence hung heavy until Keller broke it with a voice like carved granite.

"It's time."

His defense minister leaned forward, wary. "You're sure, sir?"

Keller nodded, eyes locked on the screen showing New Egypt's crumbling regions. "We didn't build this to sit on it forever. We hoped we'd never need it."

He turned toward the vault at the end of the room—sealed, locked since before the first bombs fell.

"But the world didn't burn quietly."

He took a keycard from his coat. Swiped it.

The vault doors hissed open, revealing an enormous digital interface, dormant for years.

"Project Phoenix Protocol," Keller said. "Activate it."

The room jolted with motion—lights flashing, engines rumbling far below, red banners rising on the screens.

"Revive every division. Launch the navy underground. Scramble the air fleet. Tell the world—New Egypt is not dead."

And beneath the earth… the Phoenix rose.

President Jonas Keller stood at the center of the war chamber, eyes locked with his cabinet, his voice carrying the weight of years in hiding.

"I know some people think I'm a hero," he began, steady and unflinching. "And I know others think they should try me for treason."

The room fell still.

"I've seen what our people are enduring. Every day, drone footage pours in—starving families, occupied towns, soldiers dying to hold what little ground remains."

He paused, letting the silence speak.

"But if we'd responded with full nuclear authority when this started, we could've plunged the entire world into World War III. New Egypt would not be the only one suffering—it would be everyone."

He paced slightly, hands behind his back.

"For seven years, our people have endured hell. And yet, they've captured forty-six percent of the country back. They've fought. They've survived."

Keller turned back to the command table. "I won't pretend this was ideal. There's no manual for apocalypse. But when we enacted Project Phoenix Protocol, we knew what it meant."

He tapped the digital console beside him. "Retreat. Rebuild. Rise."

"And yes… it meant leaving our people alone in the storm. That's a burden I carry. One I'll carry forever."

He looked every man and woman in the eye.

"But now the storm is ending. Today, we send aid. Weapons. Supplies. Firepower. The New Egyptian army returns—not to survive, but to liberate."

He raised a fist.

"We will take our country back. And we will avenge the fallen."

The bunker erupted—cheers, salutes, fists in the air.

And deep beneath the ground, the machines of war began to move.

The MRAP swerved as the shell slammed into the front, the engine block erupting in flames. Robert cursed, wrestling the wheel as thick black smoke poured into the cab. "Everybody out—now!"

The vehicle groaned as it tipped sideways, landing hard with a metal screech. Maya kicked the door open, dragging Ethan with her. Bridget rolled out behind them just as Robert jumped free—moments before the second shell hit.

BOOM.

The explosion threw hot metal and dust into the air, flipping the vehicle onto its roof as fire consumed it.

They didn't look back. They ran.

Gunfire tore up the pavement behind them—then the roar of a helicopter filled the sky. The chopper came in low, blades slicing the air, rockets locking on.

Robert spun. "I left the launcher…"

They ducked behind the cracked walls of a rundown motel. Plaster shattered as bullets rained down from above. Bridget shielded Maya with her body. Ethan covered the flank, breathing hard.

Robert pulled his LMG, eyes burning. "I've got one mag left."

Maya grabbed his vest. "Dad, no—"

He didn't listen.

He stepped out, took a knee behind a broken wall, and aimed up. The chopper circled, lining up for a kill.

Robert braced, gritted his teeth… and opened fire.

BRRRRRRRTTTTTT.

The LMG roared as he traced the cockpit and engine with precise, punishing fire. The glass cracked. Smoke hissed from the tail. Then—boom.

The chopper spiraled out of the sky and crashed in a burst of fire behind the treeline.

Silence.

Robert stood there, rifle smoking, sweat pouring down his face.

"No launcher," he muttered. "No problem."

Bridget walked up, stunned. "That was insane."

Maya looked back at the burning wreckage of their MRAP, eyes watering. "We lost our truck."

Robert put a hand on her shoulder. "We still have each other."

Inside the dimly lit motel room, Maya, Ethan, and Robert caught their breath. The echoes of gunfire still rang in their ears, but they knew this was just a brief respite. Robert leaned against the wall and wiped the sweat from his brow. "That was too close," he muttered.

Ethan nodded, catching his breath. "But we made it out. Again."

Robert glanced at them, determination in his eyes. "We need to link up with the resistance cells. It's time for the final push toward their stronghold."

After a brief rest, they set out on foot, moving quietly through the broken city streets toward the heart of downtown. They soon found themselves linking up with the resistance cells that had surrounded the stronghold. The resistance leader, John, a grizzled veteran, spread a map out on a table and briefed them.

"Not so fast," John said. "This won't be easy. They've got layered defenses. It's going to be like a raid in a video game—several high-stakes, deadly missions to take over their entire base. We'll need all the resistance we can muster, and we might even have to call the army out of their bunkers."

John handed each of them a radio. "Here, these will let you call in airstrikes. Especially you, Robert's family. We've been watching you. I'm sure the government's been watching you. You've pulled off some extraordinary things as a family. It's commendable."

John saluted them, and Robert returned the gesture with a firm nod. "We're ready."

With their new mission clear, they stepped out of the motel, ready to take on the final and most crucial battle of their lives.

Bridget quickly instructed the others on how to use the military radios, a skill she had honed while moving from one resistance camp to another in her solitary days. With a determined nod, they rallied the surrounding resistance fighters. The time had come.

Suddenly, the sky above them roared to life as military transport planes emerged from hidden bunkers. They dropped crucial supplies—medical kits, military aid, and even tanks—onto the ground, reinforcing the resistance and providing relief to civilians.

Moments later, like falcons unleashed from the depths, military jets soared into the skies. They targeted enemy prison camps across the country, freeing captives and bolstering the ranks of the resistance. They also provided crucial air cover, striking enemy fortifications and aiding the push toward the stronghold.

As drones buzzed overhead, delivering real-time intelligence and support, the family knew they were no longer alone. The tide was turning, and the final battle to reclaim their home had begun.

A clear message crackled through the resistance radio. "This is President Jonas Keller. I know many of you may be angry with me for everything that has gone wrong in the past seven years. It may feel like your government abandoned you. But we knew that if we fought back with full nuclear force, we could have plunged the world into a greater catastrophe. We had to bide our time and build our strength while the worst happened above ground.

Now, our military is stronger than ever. Our nation is stronger than ever. With your help and the equipment we've prepared, we will take back our country and drive every invader out. I've been watching, and I know all of your sacrifices. You will all be remembered and rewarded, should you survive?" "To appease my dissenters, I will be stepping down after the war is over, and everyone has been acknowledged per our constitution." Resistance and civilians alike cheered, albeit halfheartedly, knowing the road ahead would still be rough.

As the resistance radio message ended, Bridget, Maya, and Ethan exchanged looks. Bridget sighed, "Well, that's politics for you. They waited this long while we struggled."

Robert nodded, his brow furrowed. "I wonder why they didn't come out sooner. If they were ready now, why not before?"

Ethan shrugged. "It's crazy. We've been fighting for survival, and they were underground planning all this time."

Before they could continue, a resistance member approached them, leading a German Shepherd outfitted with a tactical vest and helmet. Maya's eyes widened in shock and joy. "It's just like Raya," she whispered, kneeling to embrace the dog.

The presence of the new companion brought a glimmer of hope, a reminder of resilience and the strength they'd found in each other.

As the resistance made their final preparations before the major attack, the leader, John, addressed the group. "Reports are coming in of airdrops to civilians. People are being freed, armed, and equipped with medicine and food all over the country. It's a great thing. They're also striking mutants with airstrikes and drones, working to clear rubble and make way for our advance."

Maya, Ethan, Robert, and Bridget approached the front lines of the massive enemy base. Unlike any other, this was truly the occupational forces' HQ. It stretched for miles on all sides. In front of them were tanks, machine gun positions, rocket launchers, drones, and snipers. As they advanced, they took cover behind a car while shots rang out from a hidden sniper.

Bridget tried to engage, but to no avail. "I can't get a hit on him. He's sticking his rifle out behind armored plates," she said in frustration. Robert attempted to flank, but the enemy's defenses were too tight.

Heavy fire was exchanged as rockets hit the ground and soared overhead. A huge, intense battle had begun. Maya and Ethan tried to find an opening, but the cover on both sides was too good, leaving them in a tense standoff as the resistance and the enemy exchanged relentless fire.

The resistance leader shouts, "RPG incoming, get to cover!" Robert yells, "They've got tanks! I really wish I had my rocket launcher right now." John calls out, "We have Javelins! Fall back to the other position and grab them!"

The family retreats, grabbing a Javelin launcher. It's too heavy for one person, so Bridget, Robert, Ethan, and Maya work together to aim and fire at the tanks, taking them out in an intense sequence.

With the tanks destroyed, they push forward, but drones begin to swarm overhead. Bridget and Maya snipe the drones with precision, while Ethan and Robert use the M249 and M4 to shoot them down, clearing the skies as they advance deeper into the enemy stronghold.

A squadron of F-35 Lightning II fighters swooped over the resistance fighters. Some of the resistance members were momentarily confused until they realized these were friendly aircraft. The jets unleashed their bombs on the front of the enemy base with a series of thunderous explosions, ripping through the defenses and twisting metal. The first line of the enemy stronghold was shattered, allowing the resistance fighters, along with Robert and his family, to surge forward in a blaze of gunfire. Ethan felt a rush of pride and excitement as they pushed ahead.

Ethan grinned and said, "That was too cool! Hey guys, did you see that? I called in an airstrike! Wow, I'm in the history books now!"

His family chuckled as they advanced. But now, an additional threat emerged: bipedal drones, more snipers, machine gunners, rocket gunners, and a wave of about ten thousand enemy troops. They found themselves inside the base, weaving through twisted metal, trying to find cover amidst the chaos of five thousand enemy soldiers and a variety of advanced drones engaging them on all sides.

Robert's family and the resistance took a higher position, with Maya and Bridget sniping from vantage points while Robert and Ethan laid down heavy machine-gun fire. Alongside the resistance leader John, they took out many drones and enemy soldiers. Despite their efforts, the battle grew increasingly intense. As they moved further into the base, they commandeered enemy equipment, which helped turn the tide slightly in their favor. Still, it was clear this would be a long and grueling battle.

"Bravo Team, infiltrate through the tunnels and hit them from behind. Alpha Team, deploy EMP grenades to knock out their defenses. Charlie Team, coordinate with the military for a ballistic missile strike on their fortifications. Move out!" John ordered.

Under the cover of night, the resistance launched its bold maneuver. EMP grenades arced through the air, detonating with a silent flash that plunged enemy electronics into darkness. At the same moment, a squad of resistance fighters emerged from hidden tunnels beneath the enemy base, catching the occupiers off guard.

As chaos erupted inside, ballistic missiles screamed down from the sky, slamming into the enemy's fortifications and ripping through their defenses. The attack threw the once impenetrable stronghold into disarray, and the resistance surged forward, turning the tide of the battle in a breathtaking, coordinated strike.

As the night wore on and the enemy lines crumbled, the resistance pressed deeper into the heart of the base. Amidst the wreckage of fallen drones and defeated occupiers, they scavenged whatever they could—ammo, weapons, and gear—fueling their determination.

John rallied the fighters, his voice resolute: "We've fought this far. I know many of you thought this day would never come, but look at us now. We will continue until we've destroyed the heart of this occupation!"

With fists raised high, Robert's family and the resistance fighters roared in unison, "Onward! Onward! Onward!" The march to reclaim their country surged ahead with unstoppable resolve.

As the night wore on, the roar of military attack choppers from New Egypt echoed through the battlefield. Streaking lines towards the center of the base, they targeted the massive concentration of enemy troops. With precision airstrikes, they decimated the enemy numbers by two-thirds, giving the resistance a fighting chance to push forward.

Amidst the chaos, as the resistance fighters looked up to see their much-needed air support thinning the enemy ranks, three choppers descended and landed in front of them.

To their astonishment, out stepped President Jonas Keller and his formidable General, Bark Daly, ready to join the fight and lead the final charge.

President Jonas Keller addressed the resistance. "I've seen you, John. I've seen you, Robert, and your family. You have changed our nation, and you will not be forgotten. You will be rewarded." The resistance fighters and Robert's family thanked the president and the general for their support. Keller continued, "I'm here because I felt it was the right thing to do—to lead my troops into this final battle. I've also heard that the Belvarian occupation leader is here, the one who started this war. I want to finish this one-on-one."

Robert responded, "We also have a score to settle with General Dragovic. I'm sure you remember him—the same general who shot Ethan and put me in that work camp."

The president nodded. "Roger that. He's all yours."

The resistance and the army pushed forward, battling floor to floor, blasting through waves of enemies and drones. The towering building echoed with the relentless sounds of gunfire and explosions. With sheer determination and firepower, they reclaimed what was rightfully theirs, proving New Egypt could stand strong without outside help.

As they reached the top two floors, President Keller and his general ascended to the very top, while Robert and his family held their position just below. The stage was set for a historic confrontation, and justice was about to be served in a way that would be remembered forever.

The hallway is quiet—too quiet. Smoke still lingers on the floors below. Walls scorched. Dried blood on the floor. The family stands before a thick steel door, the last barrier between them and the man who shattered their lives.

Robert steps forward, gripping the crowbar tight. His hands are calloused, bleeding. He jams it between the frame and the warped metal, breathing heavy.

He doesn't speak. Doesn't need to.

The steel groans under pressure.

Then—

GENERAL (O.S.)

(voice booming from inside)

"Don't open that door. If you open that door… it'll be the last thing you do."

Silence. The kind that squeezes the air from your lungs.

Robert doesn't flinch. Doesn't even blink. He looks back at Bridget, Maya, and Ethan—each one locked in, ready.

He turns back to the door.

ROBERT

"Then I'll die knowing I brought you down with me."

With one last pull—CRACK—the door tears open just an inch.

TAT-TAT-TAT-TAT-TAT!!!

RRRRRRRRRRRRR!!!

A tidal wave of gunfire erupts from inside. Muzzle flashes light up the room beyond. A mini-gun spins to life like thunder. The family dives out of the way, sparks flying, chunks of the wall ripped to shreds.

ETHAN

"Turret! Down! Down!"

Maya slides behind a beam, pops a flashbang. It clanks against the floor.

BOOM!

Screams. Confusion.

BRIDGET

"Now! Move!"

Robert and Maya rush in, firing. Ethan covers from the rear, every shot deliberate. Bridget sweeps the flank, cold and surgical.

Smoke fills the air. Bodies drop. Blood paints the walls.

And through the haze, the general bolts toward the back room, shouting:

GENERAL

"You're not gonna get away with this! You hear me? You're coming for me? I am the storm!"

Robert yells back,

"Not anymore."

The gunfire dies down. Smoke drifts like ghosts over the carnage. Dozens of bodies lie still—twisted, broken. The whirring mini-gun finally sputters to silence. Sparks pop from the shredded walls.

The general scrambles through the back doorway, wounded but still defiant.

Robert storms after him, blood on his face, weapon shaking with fury.

GENERAL

"You think this changes anything?! You think this makes you better than me?"

Robert steps into view, shouting with a voice that echoes through the shattered compound:

ROBERT

"This isn't just about what you did to me! You dragged me to a prison camp, brutalized me, shot my son, threatened my daughter—

But that was just my hell.

You nuked our cities! You butchered civilians! You turned this country into a graveyard—

for no damn reason.

And now you want to act like you were right?"

He raises his rifle, eyes burning.

ROBERT (CONT'D)

"We're not here for revenge.

We're here to end you.

For us.

For every soul you silenced."

The general stumbles back, fury twisted into fear.

The general stumbles, bleeding, cornered near a cracked window. He reaches for a sidearm—but Robert is already there, rifle raised.

Then, he lowers it.

Sets it down on the floor.

ROBERT

"No... I'm not just gonna shoot you."

(beat)

"We're gonna finish this. Man to man."

The general scoffs, trying to stand taller, but he's swaying.

BRIDGET

(stepping forward, voice shaking)

"Are you serious?"

(then, venom in her voice)

"You're a worthless human being. What you did to my son… to my husband… I could shoot you right now."

"But that'd be too easy."

"You don't deserve mercy. You don't even have a soul."

The general speaks—but Maya cuts him off, voice raw.

MAYA

"You brutalized our dad. You shot my brother and left him there to die. Then you dragged our father to a prison camp like he was nothing."

"You want to act like we're the problem? We were kids—watching cartoons in our living room when your nukes fell."

"You took everything from us… and still think you're the hero."

"You're not. You're the disease."

The general's lip quivers. His hand tightens on his sidearm.

Ethan steps forward. There's no fear in his eyes. Just icy fire.

ETHAN

"I remember when you shot me."

(beat)

"I remember every second of it."

"And today—

You're gonna pay."

The general steadies himself against the wall, blood dripping down his side. His voice wavers, but there's still defiance behind it.

GENERAL

"You think I care what you say?"

(shakes his head)

"I never claimed to be a good man. We followed our commander. He told us you people needed to be destroyed… annihilated."

"And we believed him. Hell, I still believe him."

(he breathes, slower now)

"Maybe I've got some doubts. Maybe I'm not proud of all of it. But I'm a soldier. I fulfilled my orders. That was my duty."

(he looks them all in the eye)

"I'm a patriot. And I'm proud of everything I've done."

"I can't take it back. I won't pretend it wasn't real. And to you… to all of you… I — I…"

GENERAL

"I can never apologize."

(he shrugs slightly.)

"Yes, there's a part of me—what you might call still human—that maybe wants to. But like I said… I followed orders."

(he looks Robert dead in the eye)

"So do what you must. I should've killed you all when I had the chance."

He turns toward Bridget, a twisted smirk forming.

GENERAL

"And Bridget… yes. I saw you. More than once. Long before I met your husband, your children."

"I spared you. Again and again."

"So tell me—who has more mercy? Me… or you?"

"Seems like we both became animals, didn't we?"

(he opens his arms slightly.)

"Go ahead. Brutalize me. Kill me. It's just my turn."

The room is silent. The air feels like it could shatter.

The general smirks, arms out, playing the victim.

Robert steps forward slowly, eyes blazing, his voice low and cutting.

ROBERT

"I've had just about enough of your crap."

"All you do is lie—lie to yourself, lie to your men, lie to the world."

"You live in a delusion. And if you want to follow that dictator…"

"Then follow him—

straight to the gates of Hell."

BANG!

The general pulls his pistol and fires.

The bullet rips past Robert's vest, scraping against his left rib. Armor cracks. Blood spurts from the flesh wound.

Robert GRUNTS—but doesn't fall.

With a sudden surge, he lunges forward, knocking the pistol from the general's hand and slamming a fist into his jaw.

They crash to the floor, fists flying—punches, elbows, knees.

The general drives his hand into Robert's fresh wound. Robert growls in pain, nearly buckling—then spins and slams his elbow into the general's nose, shattering cartilage.

They tumble, rolling through shattered glass and blood. The general grabs Robert's throat, but Robert powers through, shoving him off and rising to his feet, heaving.

Before the general can react, Robert grabs him, lifts, and slams him down hard, bone-cracking.

The general cries out—his arm twisted under him, possibly broken.

Robert stands over him, blood dripping, chest rising and falling.

The general howls as his arm bends at a sick angle beneath him. He's down—but not done.

With a sudden twist of his legs, he kicks Robert in the stomach, sending him staggering back.

CRACK—Robert's head smashes against the wall. He slumps to the floor, dazed, blood trickling from his temple.

BRIDGET

"I've got to help him—"

She steps forward, gun raised.

ROBERT

(groggy but firm)

"No… Bridget. No."

ETHAN

"Dad—come on!"

MAYA

"Let us help you!"

ROBERT

(pushing himself up, voice shaking but steady)

"I have to do this… for us."

He locks eyes with them—bleeding, bruised, barely standing—but resolute.

ROBERT

"No more running. No more waiting. I finish this."

He turns back to the general, fists clenched.

The family doesn't move—but you can feel them behind him, watching, ready, hearts pounding.

The general, wheezing on the ground, reaches out with his good hand and grabs his broken arm.

CRACK.

He resets it with a sickening snap, screaming through clenched teeth.

GENERAL

"I'm not done yet."

Robert pulls himself upright, eyes blazing.

He throws a punch—it connects. The general snaps back with a fist to Robert's jaw. They grapple again, fists flying, bodies slamming into walls, sweat and blood flying with each blow.

Then—the general sees it: a rusted steel pipe on the ground.

He grabs it.

THWACK!

It slams into Robert's side.

THWACK!

Across the back.

THWACK! THWACK! THWACK!

Robert drops to a knee, coughing blood.

Then—the kicks.

BOOM! BOOM! BOOM!

The general roars, kicking Robert repeatedly, a brutal rhythm of hate.

BRIDGET

(tears in her eyes)

"I can't… I can't just stand here—"

She grabs a nearby pipe, storms in, and slams it across the general's back.

CRACK!

Bridget (furious)

"Don't you ever touch my husband again!"

The general spins, dazed—and Robert pushes himself up, grabbing the general's arm mid-swing, trying to bend it back again, teeth clenched.

The general growls, muscles resisting—but before he can break free—

MAYA

(sprinting in, shouting)

"No more!"

She dives low, grabs the general's leg mid-kick, holds it tight, throwing him off balance.

Robert shouts, surging with everything he has left.

The general, now soaked in blood and sweat, roars—unnatural rage twisting his face. It's like something dark fuels him, something deeper than pride.

He kicks Maya off him, sending her crashing into a metal cabinet.

MAYA

(grunting, dazed)

"I'm okay… I'm okay."

The general rises, chest heaving, eyes locking onto Bridget.

He charges.

He throws a punch.

Bridget blocks.

Another—she blocks again.

A third, fourth—she parries, standing her ground, eyes blazing.

Then—a brutal backhand.

SMACK.

She flies back, hits the floor—but rolls through it, getting back up with blood on her lip, fire in her eyes.

BRIDGET

"You're not laying another hand on my family."

She rushes him.

They trade blows—a brutal, primal boxing match. Fists slam into ribs, faces, arms. The general swings wildly, but Bridget fights tight, trained, relentless.

She ducks, landing a hard jab to his gut.

A right hook. A left.

The general stumbles—then grabs her hair.

Bridget, blood dripping from her nose, eyes burning, spots a wooden chair nearby.

Without hesitation, she grabs it.

WHAM!

She slams it into the general's back. The top splinters.

WHACK!

Another strike—a leg snaps off.

CRACK!

She grips one of the remaining legs like a bat and swings it over and over again, driven by rage, love, and desperation.

But the general keeps coming.

Barely flinching.

Bridget screams, tears in her eyes, swinging the last leg—

WHAM!

He grabs it mid-swing.

Then with one swift motion, he yanks the seat of the chair from the wreckage and slams it into Bridget's face.

She collapses.

GENERAL

(breathing heavy, voice dark)

"You cannot defeat me."

"You. Cannot."

He stands over her like a monster, bloodied but defiant.

The room holds its breath.

Maya, bruised and breathless, turns—her heart stops.

Robert lies unconscious.

Bridget isn't moving.

Her chest tightens.

MAYA

(quiet, trembling)

"…You hurt my parents."

Her eyes burn. Her fists clench.

MAYA (CONT'D)

"Now you're going to die."

She grabs a fallen axe from the rubble and charges, screaming.

She swings—but her footing slips. The axe flies from her hands, clattering across the floor.

The general picks it up, turning to her with a cold smirk.

GENERAL Varnak

"That was cute."

"You might be a newly trained soldier now… but you're still not a general."

"If your parents couldn't beat me, what chance do you have?"

(steps closer)

"To me, you're still that little girl crying over your brother's body."

Maya shakes with fury.

She rushes him, trying to shove him—but he's too big.

He grabs her by the shoulders and slams her to the floor.

She groans, rising again, fists raised.

She swings—he dodges.

SLAM.

He throws her down again.

But Maya doesn't stop.

She rises a third time, barely breathing.

With a scream, she launches one last punch—right into the general's eye.

The impact isn't what brings him down.

His boot hits a chunk of fallen debris behind him—he trips, stumbles, and crashes to the floor.

A beat.

He tries to rise—but for the first time, he's vulnerable.

Maya stares at him, panting, eyes wide.

The dust settles. Maya stands over the fallen general, panting, fists trembling.

Behind her, Robert groans. Bridget stirs.

They both sit up, dazed but slowly returning to awareness.

ROBERT

(weak but determined)

"No… Maya. Stop."

He forces himself to his feet, wincing through pain.

ROBERT (CONT'D)

"I have to finish this."

He limps forward, reaches down, and grabs the general by the collar—dragging him across the room, just as Robert had once been dragged to that very spot in the prison camp.

The general stirs. Bruised, bloodied—but still not done.

GENERAL

(grimacing, laughing)

"You still can't kill me."

Then—he lunges.

They brawl again, rolling across the floor—punches flying, teeth gritted. Every movement is raw, savage, desperate.

BRIDGET

(raising her weapon)

"I'm ending this!"

ROBERT

"No! Stand down!"

"This ends man to man."

Robert draws his knife and plunges it into the general's side.

But the general growls, pulls the blade out, and slashes—slashes—slashes, cutting deep into Robert's shoulder and chest.

Ethan, watching from the side, eyes wide, heart pounding.

His vision tunnels. He decides.

Unnoticed, he grabs Maya's bolt-action sniper rifle, slides in a 30-06, 180-grain green tip round, and chambers it with a loud click-clack.

He lifts it. Aims.

BANG.

The general jerks violently—a bullet through his chest.

He collapses. Finally still.

Robert stumbles back, stunned.

ROBERT

"Ethan… what did you do?"

ETHAN

(tears in his eyes, voice steady)

"I couldn't watch it anymore."

"I can't lose you. I can't lose Mom. I can't lose Maya."

"I'm not dying today. And I'm not getting shot again by him."

"I've waited so long for this moment."

"This fight went on too long… and I had to end it."

Silence.

Then—Robert nods slowly.

And the family stands together, bloodied… but finally free.

The general's body lies motionless, the last breath of violence fading.

Maya drops her rifle and runs to Robert, throwing her arms around him.

MAYA

(sobbing)

"Dad… I thought I lost you."

"Mom… I thought I lost you, too."

"I love you. I'm so glad we survived."

She glances at the general's lifeless body.

MAYA (CONT'D)

"And I'm glad Varnak is down. But… you know, they say revenge isn't as sweet as we think."

"Still, the world's a better place without a monster like him."

ROBERT

(softly)

"You're right."

Bridget steps forward, hugging Maya tightly.

BRIDGET

"I love you too, Maya. So much."

Robert turns to Ethan, eyes full of pride and pain.

ROBERT

"Ethan… I know you had to do it. You showed maturity—not just skill."

"You're only eighteen, but you had to grow up fast."

"In the heat of it all, we let our emotions run wild. We let our hatred talk for us."

"But you—"

(puts a hand on his shoulder)

"You made the call that needed to be made. I'm proud of you, son."

Ethan doesn't speak—he just hugs his dad. Bridget joins them. They hold each other tightly, tears in their eyes.

And after a long, quiet breath… they wipe their tears, gather their things, and walk down the stairwell.

GROUND FLOOR – MOMENTS LATER

Dust still hangs in the air. The building groans, cracked and wounded by war.

As they step outside into the cool evening air—

They freeze.

Standing before them—wounded, trembling, but very much alive—

The family emerges from the building; the sky is dimming into twilight.

They stop in their tracks.

Standing just beyond the clearing—rifle slung over his shoulder, jacket torn, eyes tired but alive—

PAUL.

Bridget stares, frozen. Her voice is barely a whisper.

BRIDGET

"…No. It can't be."

Paul looks up. Their eyes meet.

PAUL

(grinning)

"Wow. You all look like you've been through a grinder."

ROBERT

(breathless, stunned)

"Yeah… we have."

"I thought you were out of the resistance. I thought you were done with this life."

PAUL

(chuckling)

"I was. But… I couldn't miss the big show."

"Guess I missed the finale, huh?"

Robert nods, eyes heavy.

ROBERT

"Yeah. We got him. The general who captured me… the one who shot Ethan."

"I appreciate you helping Maya find me. And… I see you found your wife."

(smiles)

"I'm glad you still have yours, too, Paul."

Bridget walks forward and wraps her arms around Paul, holding him tight.

BRIDGET

"I'm so glad you're alive."

"You were an excellent friend to this family."

"Thank you—for everything. For helping Maya… for getting Robert back. For getting them through Jericho."

"I know it couldn't have been easy."

Paul nods, emotion brimming beneath his calm exterior.

PAUL

"We do what we have to… for the people who matter."

The camera pulls back slowly.

The family, reunited.

The resistance is rising.

And the long, withering road… finally passed them.

President Jonas Keller stands silent, the weight of everything pressing on his shoulders.

A young officer approaches, whispering.

OFFICER

"Sir… they made it. Robert. Bridget. Maya. Ethan. They're alive."

Jonas breathes a long, steady sigh, one hand pressed to his chest. Relief flickers across his battle-hardened face.

He turns toward a heavy steel door. His general stands beside him, hand on his holster.

Without another word, Jonas pushes it open.

Inside, at the far end, seated smugly in a lavish chair, is the dictator—the one who started it all. The man who brought ruin to New Egypt.

Jonas steps forward slowly, deliberately. Every step echoes.

JONAS KELLER

"You nuked my nation."

"You killed thousands of our people. Bombed our cities for no reason."

"You turned children into mutants with your radiation. Poisoned our water. Shattered our land."

"And you forced the people of New Egypt to live like scavengers."

(steps closer)

"But I was smarter. Ten moves ahead. Playing ten-dimensional chess while you played checkers."

"We built underground. We survived."

DICTATOR

(laughing bitterly)

"You're a coward. You were hiding."

JONAS KELLER

(snaps)

"Don't gaslight me."

"You're evil. You brainwashed millions to believe they should exterminate New Egyptians.

DICTATOR Thalor

(snarling)

"And now… You will be."

"I never thought we'd actually come to fight."

JONAS KELLER

(voice low, final)

"Neither did I."

"But now… It's over."

In one smooth motion, Jonas charges.

BAM.

He slams into the dictator, driving him backward. The dictator stumbles, trips—

CRASH.

They smash through a glass window.

The dictator screams—falling to his death.

Jonas stands there at the shattered edge, wind in his hair, unflinching.

No speeches. No dramatics.

Just justice.

He turns to his general.

JONAS KELLER

"Let's walk."

And together, they descend the steps toward a new future.

Jonas Keller wipes the blood from his hands, breath steady, gaze fixed. The dictator is dead—but the war is not.

His general walks beside him, silent.

They stop before the elevator. No press. No celebration. Just duty.

Jonas turns to him, voice low and resolute.

JONAS KELLER

"It's time."

The general stiffens, nods.

GENERAL

"What kind of attack are we launching?"

Jonas doesn't hesitate.

JONAS KELLER

"Full conventional strikes on the sixteen other nations that supported this invasion. Take out their silos, their power grids, their fleets."

He pauses.

JONAS KELLER (CONT'D)

"As for the capital of New Egypt… one nuke might not be enough."

"Send five. If one fails… the other four will bury them."

The general blinks—only for a second—then nods again.

GENERAL

"Understood. I'll relay the order now."

Jonas looks forward, the weight of every soul lost behind his eyes.

JONAS KELLER

"No more mercy. No more waiting. This war ends today."

They continue walking—toward the command center, toward his people… and toward history.

Five nuclear-tipped ballistic missiles pierce the heavens, trails of fire behind them. Each one separates mid-flight, releasing hypersonic glide vehicles locked onto a single target: the Belvarian Occupation Nation's capital.

Belvarian occupation command center–moments later

Sirens blare. Chaos.

TECHNICIAN

"We have five inbound—repeat, 5 nuclear missiles inbound!"

COMMANDER

"Scramble air defenses! Scramble everything! Get interceptors in the air—NOW!"

Panic. Alerts. Screens flash red.

INT. STRATOSPHERE–MOMENTS LATER

Interceptor missiles rise to meet them—four detonate mid-air.

BOOM. BOOM. BOOM. BOOM.

A chain of fiery explosions lights up the sky.

But the fifth?

It breaks through.

BELVARIAN OCCUPATION CAPITAL–SECONDS LATER

The final missile hits the ground.

A blinding white flash. Then silence. Then the roar—

MUSHROOM CLOUD.

Rising high into the sky.

Just like the ones that had fallen on New Egypt.

GLOBAL BROADCAST–NEWS ANCHORS STUNNED

: A nuclear strike has hit "The enemy capital…"

"…one of the five missiles broke through defenses…"

"…a clear message: you nuke one, you get nuked M.A.D. Those are the rules."

VARIOUS LOCATIONS–GLOBAL STRIKES UNDERWAY

Conventional forces sweep in. Jets scream through the skies, destroyers launch missiles, ground troops breach enemy strongholds.

Within hours, the sixteen other nations begin surrendering, flags lowered, forces disarmed.

Belvarian Occupation PARLIAMENT–LEADERS IN TEARS

"We never wanted this war. It was him. The dictator… he lied to us all."

New Egypt–DAYBREAK

The sun rises on a broken nation—but a free one.

Jonas Keller didn't launch the strikes in vengeance.

He launched them as a president fulfilling an oath—to protect his people. To end the war. To restore his homeland after seven years of occupation, nuclear devastation, and genocide.

And he did.

Justice wasn't delivered with cruelty—but with clarity.

The war was over. NATIONAL SQUARE–New Egypt–THREE WEEKS LATER.

The skies are clear. Banners wave. The flag of New Egypt flies high above a rebuilt government building. Thousands gather—veterans, survivors, citizens free for the first time in years.

President Jonas Keller stands at the podium, medals gleaming on his chest. Behind him stand Maya, Ethan, Bridget, and Robert—not in military uniforms, but in civilian clothes, heads high.

Jonas looks out over the crowd.

JONAS KELLER

"These four brave souls… are not career soldiers."

"They were a family. A family that once had normal lives. But everything changed when war reached their doorstep."

(beat)

"And instead of cowering—they stood tall."

"They didn't fight for glory. They fought to survive. And in surviving… they resisted."

He turns, looking at the family behind him.

"This family represents the spirit of New Egypt."

Bravery. Sacrifice. Patriotism. Righteousness. law. Order.

And the unbreakable will to endure."

The crowd stirs with emotion. Some cheer. Others wipe tears.

JONAS KELLER

"And that is why I will fulfill my promise—to honor all who fought. Every soldier. Every citizen. Every soul who gave something in this Black Autumn War."

"Your names will go down in history."

He pauses, then nods toward the family.

"But this family… this family is the model of everything we stood for."

"Maya and Ethan—children forced to become warriors. Fighters who stood in the face of monsters and rose as champions."

"Bridget—separated, relentless, holding the line alone through the darkest nights."

"Robert—a father, a prisoner, a protector—who never gave up on his family, or his country."

"They didn't just survive… they changed the course of this war."

He steps forward and pins medals on each of them, one by one.

The crowd erupts into a thunderous standing ovation.

NATIONAL SQUARE–New Egypt–DAY

The wind calms. The crowd holds its breath.

President Jonas Keller stands tall at the podium, the weight of history in his voice.

He turns to face the four figures beside him—Robert, Bridget, Maya, and Ethan—standing shoulder to shoulder.

JONAS KELLER

"Today, I bestow upon you the highest honor this nation can give."

He steps down, one box in each hand.

"The Medal of Freedom."

"And the Medal of Honor."

He places the medals—both of them—on Robert's chest.

KELLER

"For leadership. Sacrifice. And protecting the spirit of this country through unimaginable hardship."

Next—Bridget.

KELLER

"For your courage. Your strength. Your resolve. You remind us that the strongest soldiers are not always on the front lines."

Then Ethan, standing proud in his uniform.

KELLER

"For your bravery in the final hour, for saving your family, and for making a decision that changed the course of history."

Lastly—Maya, still bloodied in the people's memory, but glowing now with peace and strength.

KELLER

"For your fire. Your determination. Your heart. You were born into war, but rose into legend."

The four medals gleam in the sun.

The crowd erupts—cheers, sobs, chanting their names.

New Egypt will remember them not just as heroes—

But as a family that never broke.

The applause softens as Robert steps forward, his voice calm, steady.

ROBERT

"Thank you. We didn't do this for recognition… we did this for our family."

BRIDGET

(softly, with tears in her eyes)

"We just wanted to survive. To see each other again. That was always enough."

ETHAN

(nodding)

"I wasn't trying to be a hero. I just didn't want to lose them. Not again."

MAYA

(quiet but fierce)

"We fought because we had to. And if we had to do it again—we would."

The crowd goes silent.

And then—a wave of applause, not loud or wild, but deep. Respectful. Lasting.

These weren't warriors chasing glory. They were a family who chose to stand when others fell.

And now, they stand as symbols of an entire nation's survival.

EPILOGUE

Bridget closed the book gently, the worn pages whispering as they came together. For a moment, she didn't speak. She simply looked at the children gathered in front of her—some sitting cross-legged on the floor, others leaning against the couch, one curled close to her side.

Their eyes were wide. Not with fear—but with understanding.

Outside the window, the evening sun dipped low over a rebuilt city. Lights flickered on along clean streets. A train passed in the distance. Life moved forward—quietly, steadily—because it could.

Bridget finally spoke.

"And that's how we survived," she said.

Her voice was calm now. Not proud. Not bitter. Just true.

"That's the story of your grandparents… and your parents. That's our story."

She paused, then added, "The story of our nation."

One of the children swallowed hard. Another hugged their knees tighter.

Bridget glanced down at the book in her hands—the same story she had lived, bled through, and almost died in. Names written inside the cover. Some are still alive. Some not.

She smiled softly, but there was weight behind it.

"That's what we sacrificed to give you the life you have now," she continued. "The schools you go to. The food on your table. The peace you wake up to."

Her gaze hardened just slightly—not with anger, but with conviction.

"So you should always appreciate it. Always protect it."

She placed a hand over her heart.

"Always put God first."

The room was silent. Even the youngest child understood this wasn't just a story.

"And always remember," Bridget said quietly, "this freedom wasn't free."

She closed the book and rested it on the table.

For a moment, no one spoke.

Then one child asked, barely above a whisper,

"Did it hurt?"

Bridget thought of smoke. Of blood. Of loss. On nights, she didn't know if she'd ever see her family again.

"Yes," she said honestly. "It did."

She reached out, pulling the children closer.

"But it was worth it."

Outside, the last light of day faded—and the nation they had fought for rested, alive because someone once refused to give up.

The story was over.

The freedom remained.

This is just the beginning. If you enjoyed this book, there's more on the way, new titles designed to inspire, inform, and elevate your journey. Explore my previously published books available on Amazon, and watch out for upcoming releases coming soon. For more insights, updates, and exclusive content, follow me on my YouTube channel and stay tuned for what's next.

YouTube Channel: **KDArsenal141**